Beckett Great Sports Heroes

Ken Griffey Jr.

By the staff of Beckett Publications

House of Collectibles • New York

H This is a registered trademark of Random House, Inc.

Published by: House of Collectibles
201 East 50th Street
New York, NY 10022

Distributed by Ballantine Books, a division of Random House, Inc., New York,
and simultaneously in Canada by Random House of Canada Limited, Toronto.

Manufactured in the United States of America
ISBN: 676-60028-x

Cover design by Michaelis & Carpelis Design Associates, Inc.

Cover photo by Tom DiPace
Back cover photos by (left to right) Tom DiPace, Kirk Schlea (2)

First Edition: April 1996

10   9   8   7   6   5   4   3   2   1

The Publisher would like to thank Dr. James Beckett
and the staff of Beckett Publications for providing the editorial and photo content of this book.

Managing Editor Gary Santaniello, Art Director Lisa McQuilkin Monaghan, Editor Mike Pagel and Prepress Coordinator Rob Barry had the
able editorial, design and production assistance of Theresa Anderson, Barbara Barry, Therese Bellar, Amy Brougher, Emily Camp,
Theo Chen, Belinda Cross, Randy Cummings, Marlon DePaula, Gail Docekal, Barbara Faraldo, Kim Ford, Mary Gonzalez-Davis, Tracy Hackler,
Pepper Hastings, Paul Kerutis, Rudy Klancnik, Benedito Leme, Sara Leeman, Lori Lindsey, Teri McGahey, Sara Maneval, Louis Marroquin,
Mike McAllister, Monaliza Morris, Daniel Moscoso Jr., Randy Mosty, Lisa O'Neill, Mike Payne, Tim Polzer, Reed Poole, Will Pry,
Fred Reed III, Tina Riojas, Susan Sainz, Judi Smalling, Jeff Stanton, Doug Williams, Steve Wilson and Mark Zeske.

Additionally, the Publisher would like to acknowledge the entire staff of Beckett Publications, which was instrumental in the completion of this book: Dana Alecknavage,
Jeff Amano, Jeff Anthony, Kelly Atkins, Claire Backus, Kaye Ball, Airey Baringer, Randy Barning, Eric Best, Louise Bird, Cathryn Black, Pat Blandford, Bob Brown, Chris Calandro,
Randall Calvert, Mary Campana, Susan Catka, Jud Chappell, Albert Chavez, Dawn Ciaccio, Marty Click, Cindy Cockroft, Gary Coleman, Laura Corley, Andres Costilla,
Brandon Davis, Lauren Drews, Julie Dussair, Ben Ecklar, Carrie Ehrhardt, Craig Ferris, Gean Paul Figari, Jeany Finch, Joe Galindo, Gayle Gasperin, Stephen Genusa, Loretta Gibbs,
Marcelo Gomes DeSouza, Rosanna Gonzalez-Olaechea, Jeff Greer, Mary Gregory, Robert Gregory, Jennifer Grellhesl, Julie Grove, Patti Harris, Leslie Harris, Mark Harwell,
Beth Harwell, Cara Hastings, Joanna Hayden, Chris Hellem, Dan Hitt, Mike Jaspersen, Jay Johnson, Eddie Kelly, Wendy Kizer, Rich Klein, Brian Kosley, Tom Layberger,
Scott Layton, Jane Ann Layton, Stanley Lira, Kirk Lockhart, Bobby Lorgeree, Lisa Lujan, John Marshall, Omar Mediano, Beverly Mills, Sherry Monday, Rob Moore,
Mila Morante, Mike Moss, Allan Muir, Shawn Murphy, Hugh Murphy, Mike Obert, Rich Olivieri, Stacy Olivieri, Wendy Pallugna, Laura Patterson, Diego Picon, Fran Poole,
Gabriel Rangel, Bob Richardson, Grant Sandground, David Schneider, Brett Setter, Elaine Simmons, Dave Sliepka, Sheri Smith, Rob Springs,
Margaret Steele, Marcia Stoesz, Doree Tate, Jim Tereschuk, Larry Treachler and Carol Weaver.

Foreword

Infinite Brilliance

Even after entering the league of
high-stakes and high pressure,
Ken Griffey Jr. has maintained
his happy-go-lucky spirit

TOM DiPACE

**The key element to Griffey's friendly personality
always has been his sincere smile.**

There's nothing like the atmosphere of Little League baseball – the enthusiasm, the hustle, the sincerity. Win or lose, the kids always seem to be enjoying themselves. As the players get older though, the game becomes more of a labor than the fun activity it used to be. Many major league players shun the fun and display a "no-smile" business-like attitude. Ken Griffey Jr. however, seems to have as much fun on the field today as he had as a boy taking his first few cuts with a 26-ounce Louisville Slugger.

Every time Cincinnati Moeller baseball coach Mike Cameron watches Junior's highlights on television, he remembers when The Kid was still just a kid.

"You know when he scored the winning run against New York [in the '95 playoffs]?" Griffey's high school coach asks. "Did you see that smile? That's a kid's smile. All I could think of was, 'That's Kenny.' "

Cameron was a key contributor to the publication you now hold. He sent us some "vintage" Griffey high school photos (several smiles, of course) and his prep stats.

Today, more than ever, Junior continues to smile. And through his love for the game and his actions on the diamond, Griffey prompts even more smiles from baseball fans all across America.

Mike Pagel

Mike Pagel
Assistant Editor

CONTENTS

Winning
is everything

Ken Griffey Jr. has fame, fortune and a loving family.
All he wants now is another shot at a championship.

By Bob Finnigan

Even with his six All-Star selections and six Gold Gloves, his well-timed homers and well-deserved honors, his superior production and superstar popularity, Ken Griffey Jr.'s career is best defined by one seventh-inning play against the Orioles last May 26.

With instinct and intensity that defied both imagination and gravity, Ken Griffey put everything on the line in a selfless act that summed all his parts — talent, courage and an unstoppable drive to win. Griffey made The Play, but in the process he sustained the fracture heard 'round the league.

Evidence of this baseball ballet of grace and ferocity, in which Griffey robbed Baltimore's Kevin Bass of certain extra bases with the game in the balance, appeared in the wall padding the next day.

About 4 feet from the ground was the imprint of Griffey's right shoe, struck so hard on the pad that the marks not only of his cleats, but of the shorter rubber turf grips as well, remained clearly visible. Lower to the right was the tear in the padding made by the cleats of his left shoe.

Griffey had hit the wall, spun off it and dug his left foot into it as he fell. The play is difficult to picture, never mind to do.

About 3 feet above the left shoe print was a mark left by Griffey's glove. Not far from there was the cupped indentation where his head hit. High on the left, almost so faint as not to be seen, was the spot his left hand hit, his arm fully extended in a futile attempt to prevent the fracture that was probably inevitable.

"The impact and the torque drove the wrist backward and twisted it," says Dr. Larry Pedegana, who helped hand-specialist Dr. Ed Almquist repair the damage a day later. "It was like the bones exploded."

Broken bones aside, Griffey held on to the ball.

"I saw the pictures in the paper," Seattle manager Lou Piniella says. "The kid was literally walking on air. I've seen a lot of great plays in baseball, but I've never seen anything like that."

It was vintage Griffey; more lore for the legend, which to that sore point had been the stuff of Cooperstown. Pre-crash, he had five seasons of .300 or better, four with 90-plus RBI. He was the 22nd player in baseball history to hit 40 or more home runs in two consecutive seasons.

In hitting 40 homers during the strike-shortened 1994 campaign to reach that plateau, he hit 22 by May 31, breaking Mickey Mantle's mark of 20 in 1956, and he hit 32 by June 30, breaking Babe Ruth's 30 in 1928 and 1930.

"Those things were neat when they happened," Griffey says. "Neat, but only

BEN VAN HOUTEN / MLB PHOTOS

Junior's game-winning run against New York in the '95 playoffs gave the Mariners and the city of Seattle something to cheer and smile about.

that. Otherwise, no big deal. And neither was getting hurt and missing a chance to add some numbers. They're just numbers. Only two things really count: family and winning."

Therein lies the secret of Griffey's amazing popularity, especially with kids. His personality edges into cult sta-

tus. As "Junior," an energetic and curious person, he is youthful, the eternal son even at age 26.

"And a good son, and brother and father to his own children," says Birdie Griffey, a proud mother. "Both my sons are that way."

Junior's loyalty to his family runs as deep as his desire to win. In private moments, his own achievements a given, Kenny focuses on his kin: wife

Melissa, who gave birth in October to daughter Taryn Kennedy to go with son Trey Kenneth; father Ken Sr., who just signed with Colorado as a coach; and brother Craig, who has struggled as an outfielder in the Seattle organization.

Griffey keeps his charitable work quiet, mostly to keep from being overwhelmed by requests for his limited time.

All-Star Success

Ken Griffey Jr. always gives the fans a good show at the midsummer classic

Junior followed his father's footsteps in becoming an All-Star MVP.

Baseball fans know that punching Ken Griffey Jr.'s name out of the All-Star ballot is just a formality, but they don't seem to mind doing it one bit.

In Griffey's six All-Star selections, he's led the American League in votes three times. All six times, he finished in the top three. His total of 6,079,688 votes for the 1994 game is an all-time record.

But those figures describe only how he got to the games. His on-field numbers while there are even more impressive.

Ken Griffey Jr.'s All-Star Votes

Year	Votes	A.L. Rank
1990	2,159,700	Second (Canseco)
1991	2,248,396	First
1992	2,071,407	Third (Ripken Jr.)
1993	2,696,918	First
1994	6,079,688	First
1995	1,204,748	Second (Ripken Jr.)

• Griffey became the first Mariner ever to be chosen as a starter for an All-Star Game and the second-youngest ever to start in one (1990).

• He hit the first home run by a Seattle Mariner in All-Star history at the 1992 game in San Diego. The blast off Greg Maddux was part of Junior's three-hit evening and sealed his grasp on the MVP Award.

The 1992 game made the Griffeys the first father-son combination to hit a home run and win the MVP in an All-Star Game. Ken Griffey Sr. did both in 1980.

• In 1993, Griffey became the first player to hit the B&O Warehouse at Baltimore's Camden Yards. He did so with a 460-foot blast during the Home Run Derby, in which he finished second to Texas' Juan Gonzalez.

• Junior won the Home Run Derby at the 1994 game in Pittsburgh, knocking seven balls into the stands to beat Fred McGriff, who clobbered five.

Ken Griffey Jr.'s All-Star Game Statistics

Year	Site	Avg.	AB	R	H	2B	3B	HR	RBI	BB	SO
1990	Chicago	.000	2	0	0	0	0	0	0	1	0
1991	Toronto	.667	3	0	2	0	0	0	0	0	0
1992	San Diego	1.000	3	2	3	1	0	1	2	0	0
1993	Baltimore	.333	3	1	1	0	0	0	1	0	1
1994	Pittsburgh	.667	3	0	2	1	0	0	1	0	0
1995	Texas*	.000	0	0	0	0	0	0	0	0	0
Totals		**.571**	**14**	**3**	**8**	**2**	**0**	**1**	**4**	**1**	**1**

* injured; did not play

"He has a reputation for not giving of himself, which is totally undeserved," says Dave Aust, the Seattle club publicist who handles just a portion of Griffey's off-field work. "Some people see him refuse to sign for them sometimes and they ignore the fact that he signs as often and as long as he can. He makes time for special things, like spending hours with handicapped kids."

Actually, Griffey manages to spend a few minutes with every kid who reads one of the local papers, *The Seattle Times*. Once a week during the baseball season, Griffey uses the newspaper as a forum to answer questions kids have about his game and life or their games and lives.

His advice is constant: Stay in school, work hard, play hard, have fun and do the right thing.

For his work in the community, Griffey received the 1994 Recognition Award from the Make-A-Wish Foundation. For his work with senior citizens, focusing on former players in the Negro Leagues, he received the 1994 A. Bartlett Giamatti Award from the Baseball Assistance Team (B.A.T).

Out of action with the fractured wrist, he chartered a plane and took a group of underprivileged children from the Seattle area to Disneyland.

"Junior is amazing, the way he stays so upbeat, especially with all he went through this year," says Jay Buhner, Griffey's close friend and partner in the outfield. "He loves baseball, but he genuinely likes people. And he understands people. Nobody puts anything over on him."

One of Buhner's favorite lines is his wish to spend a day as Griffey.

"I mean that I'd like to have his abilities for a day, but not his life," Buh-

Junior's a star in baseball's ballet of grace and ferocity.

ner says. "Everyone thinks he's got it easy. First of all, he works at his game a lot more than people think. Second, do you realize he can never get up in the morning and have what we'd consider a normal day?

"People are after things from him

all the time and he just deals with it. He takes care of more people in more ways than anyone will ever know. He can't go out to eat a simple meal without being asked for his autograph, not once but dozens of times. Popularity has its price, and he pays it every day.

That's not easy, and although he raises a gripe every now and then, he never really complains."

Griffey's attitude harks back to the day in 1969 when Muhammad Ali visited Harvard to give a speech on his philosophy of life. He wrapped it up with one of his poems, a quickie couplet.

"Me?" The Greatest intoned, smiling broadly. "Wheeee!"

Griffey, who saw kids buy a million candy bars named for him as a rookie in 1989, is oodles more "Wheeee!" than "me." After Game 3 of Seattle's amazing playoff comeback over the Yankees, the media pressed him for insights. Griffey hit five homers in that series, and he made it clear that his bat was doing all the talking.

"You gotta talk to the other guys — Edgar, Tino, Jay, Randy," he told re-

porters. "They did it tonight. They've been doing it almost every night. We got us a team here. No one man wins a game, not even a great pitcher like Randy Johnson or Greg Maddux."

Buhner often speaks about Griffey's team attitude and how he actually runs interference for the entire Seattle squad.

"Everyone focuses their major demands on him and it lets the rest of us concentrate on our games," Buhner says. "He handles all the jazz off the field so effortlessly, then goes out and excels."

Griffey's team spirit, so much an unthinking part of his simultaneous

Griffey got an up-close look at both the ball and the wall in 1995. However, it was Griffey's contact with the wall that caused the most devastating damage, a fractured wrist that kept the All-Star slugger out of the lineup for 73 games.

crash/catch off the bat of Kevin Bass, went on the line — the bottom line — last winter. He offered to defer a chunk of his $7 million salary so the Mariners could sign a helpful free agent or two.

At an interest rate that would make a shylock blush? "No interest," Griffey says. "Money isn't important. Winning is."

Brian Goldberg, Griffey's agent, confirms the tale: "He actually made

the offer twice."

Mariners president Chuck Armstrong says the club was prohibited from taking Griffey up on his offer.

"It is greatly appreciated," Armstrong says. "Junior's desire to win is just one of the reasons we want to keep him a Mariner for his entire career. But when we checked to see if we could rearrange his contract to defer money, we were told the union would not allow it,

Junior's Achievements

Ken Griffey Jr.'s major league statistics

Year	Team	Avg.	AB	R	H	2B	3B	HR	RBI	BB	SO
1989	Seattle	.264	455	61	120	23	0	16	61	44	83
1990	Seattle	.300	597	91	179	28	7	22	80	63	81
1991	Seattle	.327	548	76	179	42	1	22	100	71	82
1992	Seattle	.308	565	83	174	39	4	27	103	44	67
1993	Seattle	.309	582	113	180	38	3	45	109	96	91
1994	Seattle	.323	433	94	140	24	4	40	90	56	73
1995	Seattle	.258	260	52	67	7	0	17	42	52	53
Totals		.302	3,440	570	1,039	201	19	189	585	426	530

and the IRS doesn't look favorably on those kinds of arrangements."

Instead, the Mariners upped the ante in the off-season, signing Griffey to a four-year contract extension worth $34 million. The new contract includes a $50,000 bonus *if* Junior manages to make the All-Star Game.

"I've always told the Mariners it's not a matter of money," Griffey said in a conference call shortly after signing the contract extension. "I've always wanted to be on a winning team, to have something to shoot for in September and early October."

Griffey's decision to stay a Mariner wasn't always a sure thing. But much of his chatter about playing elsewhere, most notably back home in Cincinnati, was disarmed when Ken Sr. signed to coach the Rockies this winter.

No matter which weapon he chooses to accompany him to the plate, Griffey typically has found success in clobbering the opposition.

"Last season turned out great, so great I might even be willing to go through what I did to have the team come out right like it did."

What he went through — the fractured wrist — temporarily sidetracked his methodical assemblage of Hall of Fame-caliber stats. Of the totals he amassed before his 25th birthday, he was seventh among hitters since 1900 with 972 hits, fifth with 172 homers and ninth with 543 RBI. Of the players ahead of him in those categories, just Orlando Cepeda (544 RBI) and Robin Yount (1,031 hits) are not in the Hall of Fame.

He was the third-youngest player (24 years, five months) to hit 150 homers, trailing just Mel Ott (23 years, six months) and Eddie Mathews (23 years, 10 months).

If the company Griffey keeps in the record books is amazing, consider the company he keeps off the field. While Spike Lee and Reggie Jackson tell him to call anytime, he chooses instead to hang out with Buhner or a select group of close friends, most of them from his youth in Cincinnati.

The company his play puts him in is different, a cross between Mays' Say-Hey enthusiasm and Mantle's powerful majesty. Projections for his future put him in a class by himself.

"I don't want to talk about any of that," Junior says. "It's history. It's what people put on me because of what I do on the field, like getting homers in eight straight games [in 1993 to tie a major league record]. It was nice, but it

doesn't beat winning. We won some last year, but we can do better, and I think we will."

To that end last season, Griffey came back from his injury several-weeks ahead of schedule, playing with a 4-inch steel plate and seven screws in his wrist. (One screw stays, but doctors removed the plate and six screws in December.)

"This team did well without Junior, but he's our best player," pitcher Chris Bosio says. "It was so quiet without him around. We missed Junior in more ways than anyone knows. He not only was the heart of this team, it's like he was the life of its party, too."

While the Mariners went 36-37 without him, their charge into the postseason did not take place until Ken returned Aug. 15. When Griffey homered off John Wetteland with two outs in the ninth on Aug. 24, the Mariners started their climb from 11-1/2 games out of first for the third-largest comeback in baseball history.

He hit .393 in nine consecutive games in early September. He hit .448 with four homers and 12 RBI in a seven-game win streak against division rivals Texas, Oakland and California later that month. He hit .391 in the division series win against New York, including five homers with six runs driven in and nine runs scored.

He started the ALCS 6-for-12 with another home run in the first three games, but was shut down with the rest of the club from there. His big playoff numbers impressed almost everyone but Junior himself. Victory, not statistical success, had been his goal.

Cleveland advanced to the World Series; Junior's team went home.

"It was disappointing, but not disheartening," he says. "We'll be back." •

Bob Finnigan covers the Mariners for The Seattle Times.

"I have money," Junior says. "What I want is to have fun. You have fun when you win. What I always hated was picking up the newspaper and seeing four or five teams in front of us. I don't ever want to go back to that. I can't tell you how much I want to win.

Whether it's his breathtaking defensive plays or his awesome at-bats, Ken Griffey Jr. certainly has lived up to his potential through his first seven seasons in the league. The following is just a sample of the many outstanding performances that have become a quintessential part of . . .

Griffey's Highlight

Though not considered a prototypical power hitter, Griffey exploded for 45 home runs in 1993, 18 more than his career-high of 27 from the previous season. Junior's power surge peaked in late July when he homered in eight consecutive games, tying a major league record shared by Don Mattingly and Dale Long. Griffey's 420-foot blast off Yankees ace Jimmy Key helped propel Seattle to a 10-3 win at Yankee Stadium during Game 2 of the streak.

MITCHELL HADDAD

Reel

Before embarking on his home-run tear in 1993, Griffey demonstrated his remarkable power during the home-run hitting contest at the Gatorade All-Star Workout preceding the 1993 All-Star Game in Baltimore. With one mighty swing, Griffey belted a pitch over the standing-room-only area behind the right-field fence, beyond the confines of the ball-park and off the B&O Warehouse outside the stadium, 460 feet from home plate. Although Griffey finished as the runner-up in the contest to Juan Gonzalez, he remains the only batter ever to hit the B&O Warehouse on the fly.

As a 19-year-old rookie, Ken Griffey Jr. made a clear statement to Mariners manager Jim Lefebvre and his coaching staff — his days in the minor leagues were over. Griffey proved himself worthy of a spot on Seattle's Opening Day roster by blazing through other teams' pitching. The Kid's veteranlike batting skills in his first spring training led him to a .359 average with two home runs and a record-breaking 33 hits and 21 RBI. Griffey also fashioned a spring training club-record 15-game hitting streak. Lefebvre's choice was easy. Ken Griffey Jr. would be the team's new starting center fielder.

Trailing the Yankees by one run in the 11th inning of the deciding game of the AL wild card playoff series, the Mariners needed a rally. And who better to ignite one than the newest Mr. October — Ken Griffey Jr.? Griffey followed Joey Cora's bunt hit with a crisp single to center. Cleanup hitter Edgar Martinez then smacked a Jack McDowell pitch into the left-field corner. Cora scored the tying run easily. Ken rounded third in a dead-out sprint and slid into home just ahead of the throw with the winning run, triggering a mad celebration among the Mariners and more than 57,000 delirious fans in the Kingdome. For the series, Junior batted .391 with five home runs, nine runs scored and seven RBI.

By Bob Finnigan

all
in the family

The Griffey clan knows well that the family that plays together, stays together

When you ask Ken Griffey Jr. what part of his outstanding baseball career means most to him, his answer might surprise you — unless you know the real Junior.

Of all the star center fielder's glittery accomplishments, his fondest memory has nothing to do with batting records, All-Star games or even the Mariners' first-ever trip to the playoffs.

"The best time I ever had in baseball was playing in the same outfield as my father," he says. "It was my dream growing up. How many kids can say they had their dreams come true, much less playing in the same big-league game side-by-side with their dad?

"I'm the only one and nothing can top that."

The response is as forceful as The Griffey Swing.

While Junior is best known as a ballplayer whose intensity is sometimes masked by his effortless skill and 1,000-watt smile, his personal focus is as a son to Ken Sr. and Birdie Griffey, as an older brother to Craig and, in more recent years, as husband to Melissa and father to son Trey, 2, and daughter Tarin, four months.

"When baseball is such a big part of several lives in one family, sometimes the lines get blurred and the game becomes part of family life," says Ken Sr., a superb outfielder and three-time All-Star in his own 19-year big-league career. "You try to separate the job aspect from the enjoyment of the sport but there's no denying that baseball is a major part of your existence.

"Now, take that times three."

By three, Ken Sr. means himself, Junior and Craig, the youngest son of Ken and Birdie.

An athlete of note in his own right, Craig concentrated on football as a defensive back at Ohio State until the Mariners tightened their links to the family and made him a 42nd-round selection in the June draft of 1991.

While Craig has not yet experienced the success on the diamond he might have had on the gridiron, the lure of joining father and brother in the game was too strong to resist.

Little wonder. The Griffeys are a unique and amazing story in baseball.

"What it took was two special and gifted people and players," says Lou Piniella, who played with and managed Ken Sr. and currently coaches Junior. "I can't even begin to think when you might see all the factors combine for us to see it again."

Incidentally, lest anyone think the sons inherited their abilities from their father only, Junior points out his mother also was a considerable athlete.

Alberta, who goes by Birdie, played several sports in high school. "Volleyball, basketball, softball," Junior says. "She even used to come out and toss a baseball with me and Craig . . . until I burned her hand with a throw one day."

When that happened, Birdie's duties as a baseball mother changed, but she's still as active as ever. She still calls Junior occasionally, warning him when she notices a hitch in his stroke.

After all, she's been studying The Griffey Swing for almost three decades.

Similar as players, Ken Sr. and Junior are also quite alike as people. The sameness was evident from the first time Junior took batting practice in Seattle's Kingdome.

"You see Junior hit and you'd swear you were watching his old man swing the bat," says Bob Harrison, the senior scout who signed Junior for Seattle. "They are alike, although Junior might have more bat speed."

Ken Sr. knew The Griffey Swing would be part of his son's abilities from the start.

"I think the last time we changed anything," the father recalls, "Junior was 9 years old."

From there, the similarities are most obvious in their personalities. Before their first game together, against Detroit in Seattle on Aug. 31, 1990, Junior told Brian Goldberg, agent to all the Griffeys, "It's really going to be weird tonight, playing with my dad."

Later, when Goldberg was driving Ken Sr. to the game, the father said, "It's really going to be weird tonight, playing with my son."

Both are easygoing and quick to laugh. Both have a serious streak, too, but they're better known for the shared sense of humor.

The humor was evident even in that historic first game. They started off by hitting back-to-back singles off the Tigers' Storm Davis, then

COURTESY OF CINCINNATI REDS

Ken Sr. later had to make several long running catches in left.

As his father jogged back to his position, Junior put his face behind his glove but his shaking shoulders betrayed his laughter.

Yet both had poignant thoughts on that first game they shared.

"When we went into the first to start the game, I didn't know what to think," Junior says. "I wanted to cry or something. It just seemed like a father-son game, like we were out in the backyard again just playing catch. But we were actually in a real game. I just stood there and looked at him. A couple of pitches even went by; I didn't watch."

"I didn't know what to expect," Ken Sr. says. "The first time up was like being a rookie again. But after the first pitch, I settled down."

The two had a bet — for dinner — on who would get the first hit. When Junior followed his dad's single with one of his own, he called it a tie.

The best example of their banter might have been their debate about the historic back-to-back homers on Sept. 14, 1990.

The next day, Junior insisted his was a better blast,

The Griffey boys (Ken Jr., right) grew up at the ballpark, with Ken Sr. always playing the proud father.

Just having his
father standing by
and looking out for
him through his
formative years
was a luxury Junior
appreciated.

like
father, like son

One night in 1990, Junior followed his father's footsteps — all the way around the bases

With Ken Griffey Jr.'s broken left wrist costing him 73 games in 1995 — about half the season — he and his father fell farther behind the Bonds clan, Barry and father Bobby, in the father-son career home run rankings.

Junior high-fived his dad, then drilled a homer of his own.

MEL BAILEY

Barry and Kenny hit homers at about the same rate last year — 33 in 506 at-bats for Bonds, 17 in 260 for Griffey — but the Bondses now lead with 587 lifetime homers.

The Griffeys rank fourth with 341, also behind Gus and Buddy Bell and Yogi and Dale Berra, tied for second with 407.

But the Griffeys hit home runs that none of the others can touch, nor is anyone else likely to for a long time. On Sept. 14, 1990, they not only hit home runs in the same game against the Angels in Anaheim, Calif., they hit them back-to-back in the first inning.

Ken Sr.'s was a 402-foot jolt to center on an 0-2 pitch from starter Kirk McCaskill. Junior followed four pitches later, getting a green light on 3-0 and slamming a 388-footer out to left.

"I kept looking at [third base coach] Bill Plummer for a sign, just to make sure the 'take' wasn't on," Junior says. "It's something I didn't think we'd ever do."

Not for lack of trying. Ken Sr.'s homer was his third in 15 games that first memorable month with Seattle, and his son had tried in vain each other time to follow up with one of his own.

When Junior greeted his dad at the plate that night, both knew he would be trying again.

"I could see it in his eyes," Ken Sr. says. "I felt for him then. I knew he would be thinking home run. I hit the first two against Oakland and Boston and I knew he had tried hard to hit one, too. Maybe too hard.

"I just sat quiet in the dugout and hoped he got a pitch he could hit, then . . . boom."

Most of the Mariners climbed to the top of the dugout steps to greet Junior, but Ken Sr. stayed behind, clapping, proud as any father would be.

"He was the first person I looked for," Junior says.

When the son got into the dugout, they looked at each other, smiled and embraced. Then the ever-present Griffey humor came in.

"It's about time," Ken Sr. told his son.

— Bob Finnigan

although Ken Sr.'s shot outdistanced his, 402 feet to 388.

"Maybe," Junior conceded at last. "But mine got out of the park faster."

Junior went on to proclaim that he had gotten out of the batter's box faster than his dad did.

"Hey," Ken Sr. replied.

"When you hit them as far as I did, you don't have to get out that fast."

When Ken Sr. joined the Mariners at the start of that memorable September, he was concerned that playing with his son would be viewed as a publicity stunt.

"This allows me to do what I want to do: play alongside Junior," he said at the time. "But if I didn't think I could still play, I would pass on that opportunity."

What is little known is that Ken Sr., at 40, outhit his son that final month of the 1990 season, .400 to .312, including a 12-game

hitting streak.

"This tops my career, better than the '76 batting race [he finished second], even better than two World Series," Ken Sr. says. "This, for me, is No. 1."

The father played 30 games with Seattle in 1991 and retired after aggravating a neck injury, but he still hung around the clubhouse.

Ken Sr. was a hitting coach for Seattle in 1992, did stints as an instructor in the minors in '93, and served as a special assignment scout to general manager Woody Woodward in 1994.

Later, when Ken Sr. left the Mariners' organization in the spring of 1995, Junior said his dad disagreed with some of the organization's minor league operations.

The father, with his usual class, refuses to discuss it, saying instead he had an opportunity to go back to school with the idea of eventually starting his

Any time there's more than one Griffey on a team, Junior has something to smile about.

own business.

That same year proved a rocky one for Craig, too. Struggling at the Double-A level, he was dropped from Seattle's 40-man roster.

Junior reacted protectively, worrying that some in the organization were "messing with Craig."

"He's a different player than I am," Junior says. "For one thing, he's faster. If they leave him alone and give him a chance, he'll develop."

Does Junior think he was overly protective?

"He's my little brother," Junior says. "The only brother I've got. Don't you think I'd be protective?"

Junior isn't the only one looking out for Craig, though.

"We have two sons we're proud of," Birdie says.

"Kenny, yeah . . . he did go beyond my expectations. The way it is with kids now, keeping them off the streets, off drugs and out of gangs can be hard — even impossible sometimes.

"But both our boys resisted all that and have grown up to be good men."

Ken Sr.'s departure from the organization gave birth to a scheme in Junior's mind wherein he, his father and brother all wind up together on their hometown team, the Reds.

"Wouldn't that be a kick?" Junior asks. "Everyone wants to go home to play. The dream comes alive."

Then the father, who might have gone with the Reds as a coach, wound up back in baseball as a coach

with Colorado. The Dream Scheme is on hold for now.

Although their father has left for the National League and the two brothers remain in the American, baseball's push for inter-league play might give them another chance to again play together.

"What Junior has done in baseball has an effect on me — has to," says Craig, a 24-year-old outfielder. "Some of it is a plus. Some of it is a minus, such as expectations put on me. People expect me to do the things not only Junior has done, but also that Dad has done. In most ways, I am more like Dad.

"Ken is in a league of his own."

When Junior was asked in October if hitting five home runs in the Division Series win against the Yankees was the highlight of his career, he gave his usual answer: Playing in the same outfield with his father was the highlight of his career.

Then, in a quiet aside, Junior added, "This wasn't even my favorite part of this year. I preferred spring training, when I had Craig with me on the team."

Family. It means more to Ken than a tape-measured blast, a game-saving catch or a series-winning run. Family means everything. •

Bob Finnigan covers the Mariners for The Seattle Times.

KIRK SCHLEA

On Aug. 31, 1990, I lived the dream that any father would give his right arm to have come true. I stepped onto a major league field with my son, Kenny, as a teammate to play a major league game.

It's still vivid to me. In my first at-bat after my trade from Cincinnati to the Mariners, I got a base hit up the middle against Kansas City. Then Kenny came up and got a base hit to right field.

He said he was just trying to hit the ball through the hole because we had a guy on first base. It was good baseball, executed by a good player.

Then when he got to first, I looked at him and he looked at me and we nodded, acknowledging that the first time up, the first time being in a game together, we got base hits. It was very special.

I'm the old pro. I can keep my emotions in check. It took him a little while to do it, but he finally decided he could play, even if his dad is here or not — that he could show his dad.

But Kenny never really had to show me anything. I always knew what he could do.

Call it genes if you want. But with the genes comes the ability to make the adjustments to hit any pitch at any time — from pitcher to pitcher, pitch to pitch — it doesn't matter to Kenny. And that's one of the most important things that he has, along with his concentration level.

Sure, he's always having fun so everything seems like it comes natural, like he isn't working. But he works very hard. A lot of people don't understand that. Then again, they don't know Kenny like I do.

I first saw both the ability to adjust and the concentration level long before Kenny got to the majors. I saw it when he was a kid, about 12 or 13, and I was his batting-practice pitcher.

I would never tell him what was coming. I would throw different pitches at him and I could see his concentration level, what he was going to do, how he was going to approach the ball.

I would throw him sliders, curveballs, forkballs, screwballs, change-ups. It didn't matter. He would make the adjustments.

It was important to see those things then, to have that knowledge, because shortly after [that] my career took me away from the Reds and Cincinnati, where Kenny, Craig, my wife Birdie and I live. I didn't get to see him play from 12 to 17. I didn't get to see him develop.

But Kenny had a good background already, growing up around Major League Baseball.

Now, I don't know just how good he can become. He really hasn't developed as a mature player yet. He's only 26 years old.

Personally, we've enjoyed our time together as teammates, then as coach and player, because our relationship is so strong as father and son.

Even when baseball took me away for so many summers, I tried to do as much as possible (with him) when there was a break in my playing for the Yankees or the Braves. That's where our being such good friends started.

So when we got to be teammates, he already understood a lot about what was going on. I explained beforehand that if and when we did become teammates, my presence could take away some of his thunder because it would be so historic and also because I could play.

FATHER'S DAY

Ken Griffey Sr. — perhaps better known as Junior's dad — shares his memories of a dream come true

By Ken Griffey Sr.

(as told to Claire Smith)

JONATHAN KIRN / SPORTS PHOTO MASTERS

But Kenny understood. I was there to do something I don't think anybody else will ever get to do again: play in the major leagues with my son. I told him, "I have never enjoyed playing so much until I got a chance to play with you. So just relax and play the game. Enjoy it, because I am, every minute of it, just playing the game with you." •

Claire Smith is a sports columnist for The New York Times.

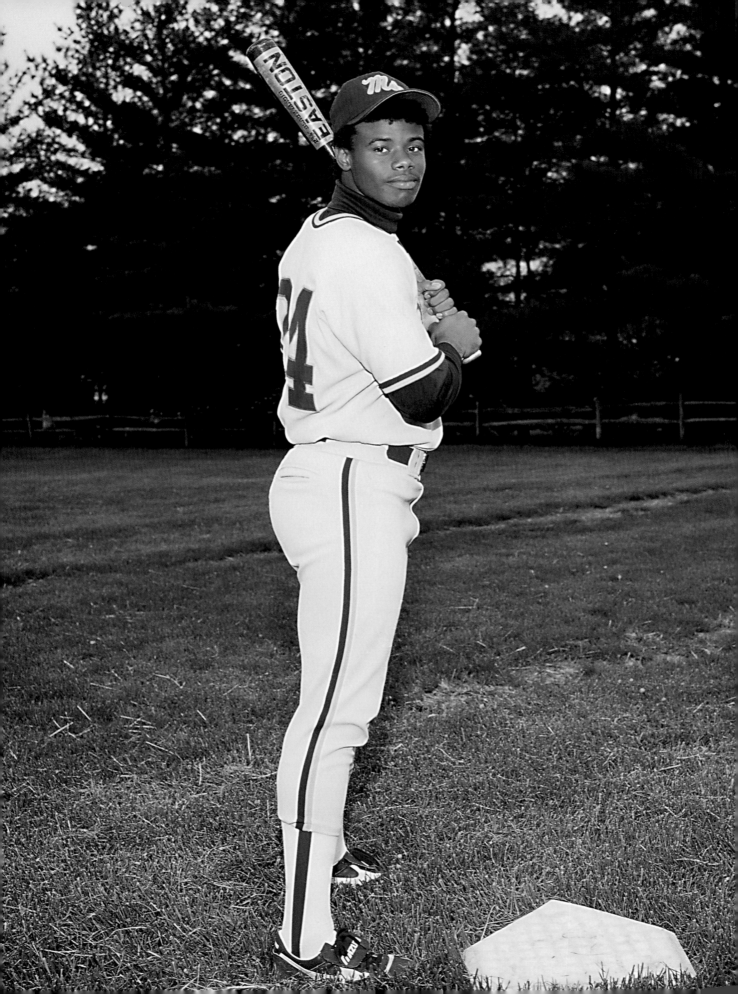

AHEAD
OF HIS TIME

Back when The Kid

was still just a kid,

everyone who saw

him play predicted

greatness would soon

follow. They were

right.

"When he was 14, he looked like he was 18. . . . If he couldn't make it, nobody could. . . . God just made this young man an athlete. . . . His talents were so ahead of any high school kid's."

The quotes about Ken Griffey Jr.'s athletic prowess as a youngster are as numerous and impressive as the home runs he used to clobber at Moeller High School in Cincinnati.

But predictably, as the spotlight increases on Griffey the major league star, the stories (or fish stories, if you will) about Griffey's youth baseball achievements continue to grow.

Home runs travel an extra 10 yards every year. Great throws from the warning track are now frozen ropes to the plate from the base of the outfield fence. And instead of going from first to third on a single to left, Ken now scores from first on a sacrifice bunt to third.

When you're dealing with a legend, it's impossible to separate fiction from fact. What we do know is this: When you look up "can't-miss" prospect in the *Baseball Encyclopedia*, Griffey's picture appears beside the definition. Of course, he's wearing a broad smile.

The smile, the swing, the arm, the speed and the uncanny ability to know where the ball was going before it got there all were part of Ken's game as a youngster. In fact, many who marveled at his skills in youth and high school leagues say nothing much has changed, except for the checks he cashes at the bank.

"When he was 14, he looked like

By Chris Haft

he was 18," explains Barry Strasser, Griffey's Knothole League coach. "He swung then like he does now; he just hits them a little bit farther. He's always had those quick wrists. People ask, 'What did you teach him?' I say, 'Not much.' "

Moeller High School's Mike Cameron has had the good fortune to coach six players who reached the major leagues: Griffey, Buddy Bell, David Bell, Len Matuzek, Bill Long and Barry Larkin. Cameron labeled Griffey as the most impressive prep athlete of the group.

"If he couldn't make it, nobody could," Cameron says. "I've been fortu-nate. I've been able to make compar-isons between them and Griffey at that age and there aren't any comparisons."

Moeller isn't your ordinary high school. For one thing, it's an all-boys school. It also boasts one of the top high school football factories in the na-tion. When you talk prep sports in Ohio, Moeller is the first topic of dis-cussion.

Jim Lippincott, who currently scouts for the Cincinnati Bengals, was the athletic director when Griffey at-tended Moeller. He remembers a young man without peer.

"God just made this young man an athlete," Lippincott says. "In the 11 years I spent there, he was the best pure athlete we had."

W atching Griffey take bat-ting practice is one of the pleasures of getting to the ballpark early (a close parking spot is nice, too).

Ken is usually good for at least a half-dozen souvenirs per session. There was one particular batting practice ses-sion that forever will stay with Strasser. And he didn't even have to pay at the gate.

Ken played for a team sponsored by a barbershop named Denny's. The field was at St. Susanna's Church in Ma-son, Ohio. Ken was 13. Strasser was his coach.

"He hit the first couple a mile," Strasser remembers.

Griffey batted .659 in his second season with Denny's while generating more legendary tales of breathtaking power.

Before one game at a place called Gower Park, a supposedly wise observer considered the field's dimensions — 322 feet down the right-field line and 410 feet to center — and remarked to Strasser before the game that nobody would hit one out. Griffey proceeded to smack a homer that landed on the street far beyond the right-field fence.

Ken graduated from Knothole ball to the Midland Redskins, one of the na-tion's most elite youth programs. Twenty-nine Midland alumni have ascended to the majors.

"We knew he was going to be really good," Strasser says. "We didn't think he would be this great."

By the time Griffey arrived at

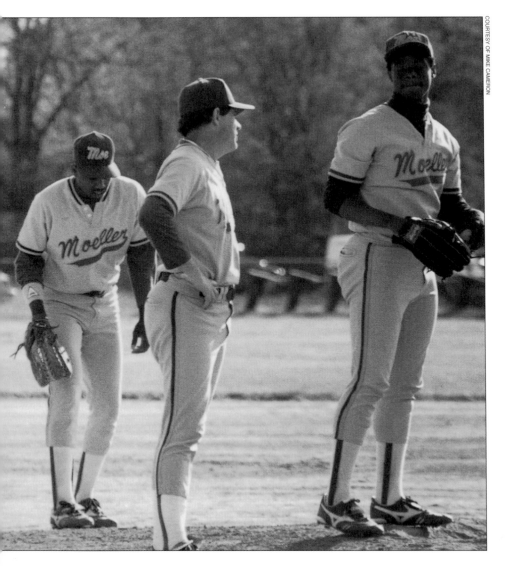

COURTESY OF MIKE CAMERON

Moeller coach Mike Cameron put Griffey on the mound in high school, but Junior was already king of the hill.

Moeller, Cameron knew all about him. Of course, when your dad plays for the hometown heroes (a.k.a. the Big Red Machine), it's hard to go unnoticed. Cameron knew his primary job with Ken was to allow this flower to blossom.

"I kind of coach on the philosophy that when a kid fails, he'll come to you for help," Cameron says. "With Ken, he really didn't fail. His talents were so ahead of any high school kid's."

Instead of refining Griffey's hitting or defense, Cameron simply tried to reinforce the teenager's sense of discipline and awareness of team concepts. "He wasn't a hard sell that way. Ken was really easy to coach," he says.

Today, every time Cameron tunes into ESPN's *SportsCenter*, it's like taking another trip down memory lane.

"The way he runs, the way he runs in the outfield, the way he ends up high swinging the bat, how he might look bad on one pitch and the next hit a tape-measure homer — it's unbelievable how many of those things we saw when he was with us," Cameron says.

While Cameron admits that Larkin, last season's National League MVP, has made big strides with his skills since leaving high school, Griffey is a mirror image of the high school phenom who tortured Moeller opponents.

When word spread that Moeller featured the "next Willie Mays," scouts came running from all over the country. Atlanta's Bobby Cox and Pittsburgh's Syd Thrift even took a look for themselves.

"It was like a circus at times," Cameron recalls. "There were more scouts in the stands than fans. Everyone wanted to watch Ken and they all called me to find out exactly where he'd be playing and when the games were. It was kinda crazy."

Most kids might have been intimi-

LOCK GRID

A sure-handed, fleet-footed receiver destined to be a football hero, Griffey Jr. instead dropped the pigskin in favor of cowhide

Rick Mirer rolls to his left and looks deep over the middle. He finds his Pro Bowl receiver streaking upfield and hits him in stride for a 70-yard touchdown. The Kingdome crowd goes bonkers as Ken Griffey Jr. raises his arms as he crosses the goal line. Another TD for the Seahawks' answer to Jerry Rice!

Don't laugh. It could have happened if Griffey had directed his athletic efforts as a youth toward the gridiron instead of the diamond.

As a junior at Moeller High School during the 1985 football season, Griffey played wide receiver and some running back for Moeller High School, traditionally one of the finest teams in the nation. The Crusaders were especially strong that year, capturing the state championship.

"He was potentially a Division I-A player if he wanted to be," says Steve Klonne, Moeller's head football coach. "He had a tremendous leaping ability and really nice speed. I remember him scoring a touchdown on a screen pass where he just outraced everybody."

Cincinnati Bengals scout Jim Lippincott, who was Moeller's athletic director at the time, recalls: "If you could throw a three-step slant to him, he could take it to the house."

Griffey's prodigious skills were evident even when he was fooling around, as demonstrated by Lippincott's memory of Moeller's Thanksgiving Day practice at Cincinnati's Nippert Stadium.

"He put the ball on a tee at the 50-yard line, kicked it and it hit an air-conditioning building outside the stadium," Lippincott testifies. "It was still going up."

Aware that a career in professional baseball awaited him, Griffey opted not to play football as a senior in 1986.

"Had we had him, we might have won it all again," Lippincott admits. "Athletically, he was so far superior to anybody we had. He could catch passes one-handed, and sometimes it was the back tip of the football. He was the difference-maker."

You can bet American League pitchers wish Ken still was catching footballs like Jerry Rice instead of smashing their offerings like, well, Ken Griffey Jr.

— Chris Haft

By Jim Caple

ADJUSTMENTS

MINOR

Ken Griffey Jr.'s two seasons in the minor leagues were little more than a pit stop on the road to major league stardom

When you're destined for a spectacular major league career, you don't have time to waste in the minors.

So Ken Griffey Jr. didn't.

Officially, Griffey spent two seasons in the minors, but really it wasn't even that much. After Seattle made him the first pick in the 1987 draft, Junior made his pro debut that June — naturally, he homered for his first hit at Bellingham, Wash., in the rookie Northwest League — and played 54 games before the summer ended.

He started the next season at San Bernardino in the Class A California League, but strained his back and spent two months on the disabled list. When Griffey was healthy again in mid-August, the Mariners promoted him to Double-A Vermont, where he played his final 17 minor league games.

If you're scoring at home, that was five months spent riding minor league buses and a mere 129 games played without big-league meal money.

Michael Jordan, mind you, played just two fewer games in his entire pro baseball career.

Though Griffey wasn't in the minors long, he nonetheless made a huge impact.

His ability was such that he hit .320 with 27 homers and 92 RBI in the two seasons and was named his

MEL BAILEY

KEN GRIFFEY JR. IN THE MINOR LEAGUES

Year	Team	Avg.	AB	R	H	2B	3B	HR	RBI	BB-SO
1987	Bellingham	.313	182	43	57	9	1	14	40	44-42
1988	San Bernardino	.338	219	50	74	13	3	11	42	34-39
1988	Vermont	.279	61	10	17	5	1	2	10	5-12
1995	Tacoma*	.000	3	0	0	0	0	0	0	0-1
Totals		.318	465	103	148	27	5	27	92	83-94

* One-game rehabilitation assignment

league's top prospect each summer. His appeal was such that Bellingham's average attendance more than doubled when Griffey played. And his name was such that one day, 20 media outlets called for an interview.

"We all sign autographs here and there," minor league teammate Paul Togneri says. "But every game it's, 'Hey, Ken Griffey! Hey, Ken Griffey!' "

Griffey also honed his baseball persona in the minors. He wasn't old enough to vote, barely old enough to drive, but even in his first year he had an ease about him — that trademark Griffey style.

Of course, some used words other than "style."

"You want to see a 17-year-old gut it out a little more," former manager of the Everett Giants Joe Strain said at the time. "You know, a kid flies out, says 'Shoot,' gets his glove and runs back out to the field. [Griffey] just sort of walks it."

Well, yeah. But how many 17-year-olds had a father in the majors?

How many had Griffey's lineage?

How many had Griffey's talent?

Junior grew up around the Big Red Machine, and later spent summers at Yankee Stadium. A series between the Bellingham Baby M's and the Everett Giants was supposed to impress him?

Not quite.

Like a genius stuck in a classroom of normal kids, Griffey probably was bored with his minor league surroundings. Of course, even in the big leagues, Ken remains in a class by himself.

Jim Caple covers Major League Baseball for The St. Paul Pioneer Press.

dated by all the fuss. Not Ken. Remember, he grew up around a major league clubhouse. "He wasn't impressed with the higher-ups of Major League Baseball being around because he grew up with it."

Occasionally the scouts wouldn't see Ken do much, since opponents often chose to pitch around the slugger. He batted .478 in both his junior and senior years despite being forced to hit mostly mistakes. Few hurlers dared challenge him. But the endless stream of intentional walks didn't obscure his excellence in the outfield.

"We used to kid the left and right fielders," Cameron says, " 'Take care of the foul lines. Kenny's got the rest.' "

Actually, Griffey's glovework might have been more awe-inspiring than his hitting. Lippincott recalls one game in which Griffey weaved in and out of some kids on a nearby field to make a catch in a driveway — sort of like the hilarious Nike spot in which Griffey

dashes across America to catch a line drive off the bat of Don Mattingly. Lippincott swears that later in the same game, Ken sped over to pluck a ball from the left fielder, who had lost it in the sun.

"He made incredible defensive plays in high school that might exceed his offensive exploits," Lippincott says.

Griffey's presence off the field was equally as impressive as his much talked about exploits on the field.

"He was as pleasant and as humble as anybody could be with the amount of success that he had so quickly," Lippincott says. "His smile was infectious."

A weekend in July 1993 demonstrated Griffey's loyalty to his baseball upbringing.

Strasser gathered many of Griffey's Knothole teammates for an unofficial

Junior's sliding technique has improved since this father-son game, but his fun-loving attitude hasn't changed at all.

Before he made the All-America team, Griffey (back row, second from left) stood out at Cincinnati Moeller.

RED MACHINE
LITTLE

From 1970 to 1978, the Cincinnati Reds won five division pennants, four National League crowns and two World Series titles.

But six players from the fabled "Big Red Machine" are having more fun watching Major League Baseball in the '90s than they had playing it — make that, dominating it — in the '70s.

That's because these six players are proud fathers watching their sons play the game today.

Ken Griffey Jr. is the player most would associate with the "Little Red Machine," but he's just one of a group of playmates who went on to follow in their fathers' footsteps. Lee May Jr., another son of a former Red, is a scout with the New York Mets, having retired as a player in that organization.

FATHER	YEARS W/REDS	SON	SON'S '95 TEAM
Pedro Borbon	'70-79	Pedro Borbon Jr.	Atlanta Braves
Ken Griffey Sr.	'73-81, '88-90	Ken Griffey Jr.	Seattle Mariners
Ken Griffey Sr.	'73-81, '88-90	Craig Griffey	Port City (Double-A)
Hal McRae	'68, '70-72	Brian McRae	Chicago Cubs
Tony Perez	'64-76, '84-86	Eduardo Perez	California Angels
Pete Rose	'63-78, '84-86	Pete Rose Jr.	South Bend (Class A)
Ed Sprague	'71-73	Ed Sprague Jr.	Toronto Blue Jays

reunion when the Seattle Mariners visited Cleveland for a weekend series. The group of about 35 coaches, ex-players and their families eagerly made the four-hour drive from Cincinnati to Cleveland, even though Strasser didn't know if Griffey would be able to devote much time to them.

Ken made the drive worth everyone's while.

On a night when Griffey hit a home run for the fifth consecutive night (he later tied the major league record of eight straight games with a homer), the Mariners' superstar made sure his guests felt welcome. When the ball that Griffey smacked was thrown back onto the outfield grass, Griffey asked teammate Jay Buhner to hand it to Strasser, who was sitting by the foul pole. After the game, Griffey entertained the group in his hotel suite, posed for pictures, signed autographs and relived old times into the wee hours of the morning.

Among the photos he signed was one for Strasser. "It was great fun growing up," the inscription began. "Thanks for letting me play for you."

Without saying a word, Strasser's broad smile said what all of his coaches would like to say, "No, Ken, thank you." •

Chris Haft covers the Reds for The Cincinnati Enquirer.

TALENT SCHOOL OF

SCHOOL OF

A school rich in history, Moeller High has been the key
that opened doors to many baseball players' dreams

The dream exists in the hearts and souls of all young baseball players.

They grow up aspiring to one day make it to the big leagues. And for athletes at Moeller High School in Cincinnati, that dream has a foundation in reality.

Glimpses at the past is all these players need for motivation toward their dreams. Since 1968, six Moeller High School baseball players have gone on to star in the major leagues.

Buddy Bell, David Bell, Len Matuszek, Bill Long, Ken Griffey Jr. and last season's NL MVP Barry Larkin all received their baseball apprenticeship in the blue and gold of Moeller High.

Through the years, head coach Mike Cameron, along with assistant coach Paul Smith, has elevated the Moeller High School baseball program into one of the best in the country. And as the Crusaders continue to win, college and major league scouts flock to the Cincinnati area in search of the next big-league prospect.

Cameron, who has a 515-230 career record at the all-boys Catholic academy, has seen a lot of talent throughout the years but never has taken any of it for granted.

"I think about it a lot and wonder 'Why me?' " Cameron says. "I wonder why I'd be so fortunate to have the opportunity to coach these good teams and be blessed with six players who have gone on to the majors."

Cameron, who is entering his 28th season at Moeller this spring, has coached the Crusaders to three state championships. In 1972, Matuszek,

COURTESY OF MIKE CAMERON

who later played for the Phillies and Dodgers, led MHS to the school's first state title. Detroit Tigers manager Buddy Bell was never a part of a state championship at Moeller, but two of his sons were. David, who spent his first season in the majors last year as the St. Louis Cardinals' third baseman, provided the punch for the Crusaders' championship in '89. And Mike, who was a recent first-round draft choice, starred on the '93 Moeller team that won it all.

But what about the more notable stars, Griffey and Larkin? Didn't they ever win a state championship?

"Some years we had better teams than our championship teams, but whether it was luck or chemistry, something just wasn't quite right," Cameron explains. "Sometimes the team that gets hot at the right time can win it all. But that never hap-

pened with Griffey or Larkin."

Cameron says that despite the recent turmoil in the major leagues, baseball remains the No. 1 sport in the Cincinnati area and especially on campus. Of this year's freshman class of 240 at MHS, Cameron says 75 have signed up to compete for the 22 spots on the team's roster.

"I think there's a sense of pride in the fact that Ken Griffey or Barry Larkin or Buddy Bell once wore the Moeller High School uniform," Cameron says. "I think a lot of kids want to be a part of that. They feel that there is a tradition to uphold."

That tradition continues again this spring as the Moeller Crusaders seek a fourth state championship and another opportunity for inspired individuals to work toward their dreams of playing in the major leagues.

— Mike Pagel

Special
DELIVERY

He wasn't expected to
arrive in the majors at age
19, but once through the
door, Junior unwrapped
a singular talent worthy of
particular attention

By Nick Cafardo

It was the end of March in 1989, and the Seattle Mariners had broken camp and were spending the final two days before the start of the season in Las Vegas for exhibition games. On the bus ride to Las Vegas from the team's training camp in Arizona, manager Jim Lefebvre already was conjuring up something cute to pull on his 19-year-old rookie, Ken Griffey Jr. After all, April Fool's Day was just around the corner.

Lefebvre sent the kid they called "Junior" a message through a coach that he wanted to see Ken in his office first thing in the morning.

Lefebvre can barely get through the rest of the story without bursting out laughing.

"You have to understand that at this point there's no reason for anyone to think one way or the other whether Junior has made the team," Lefebvre says. "He came into my office, and I start going into this long speech about how tough it is to play in the big leagues, and that just a few players have the maturity and the poise to be able to get here and stay here for a long period of time. I really laid it on. It got to the point where I know Junior was agonizing inside, thinking he was going to go back to the minors.

"I could see it in his face, and the more I talked the more I could see in his face that he was buying this. Just when I was getting to the bottom line, I popped up a little bit and said, 'Junior, you're my center fielder!'

"His jaw and his mouth just dropped," Lefebvre recalls. "I had him going pretty good. That was fun. Watching his reaction to being told he was in the big leagues is a long-lasting memory of mine. I knew then we were dealing with something very special. And maybe I treated him that way, and others resented it during the season. But the one thing is, I didn't want to break this kid's spirit. I just wanted him to have fun all through the year. People thought I treated him special. That's because he was special."

He was 19 years old and just out of rookie ball. Nobody gave Griffey much of a chance to make the Mariners' roster that year, but he took

spring training by storm, hitting .359 with two homers and 21 RBI, and fashioned a 15-game hitting streak. His 33 hits were a team spring training record.

He already was making circus catches in center field. He irritated some players, especially veterans, because he wore his cap turned backward, and his uniform sometimes hung out of his pants. Other than his dad, Junior's idol was Rickey Henderson, which explains the inspiration for some of his early flash. Everywhere he went that year, he was reminded of who his father was. Ken Griffey Sr., still with the Cincinnati Reds then, was answering questions about his son and the possibility of playing alongside him before he retired.

There also were premature comparisons to Willie Mays, and suggestions that Junior would become the greatest player who ever lived.

He was standing near the batting cage in spring training one day, looking quite comfortable, when Lefebvre asked him, more as a joke than anything else, "Junior, how many spring trainings is this for you?" Expecting to hear that it was his first, the surprise response was, "This is my 12th. I spent a lot of spring trainings with my dad in New York and Cincinnati and Atlanta."

It then hit Lefebvre and his coaching staff that they were dealing with more than a mere 19-year-old ballplayer. Hardly overwhelmed, Junior was as natural in his surroundings as any veteran player.

"I watched my dad play for years," Junior told reporters in July of that year. "I talked to him every day about the game. There isn't one thing I've seen so far that he hasn't told me about beforehand."

But Lefebvre wasn't convinced Griffey should stick with Seattle until the last week of spring training. Until then, general manager Woody Woodward told Lefebvre it was his decision.

"I've fallen into the same trap everyone else does — you see a young kid in spring training and you fall in love with him," Lefebvre explains. "After all, spring training is made for that situation. But I always learned that you tell a lot about a guy by what he does in that last week. That's when pitchers start to get ready for their first start of the regular season, and they're much more serious. If a kid doesn't drop off too badly, then he's for real.

"On this particular day, Rick Sutcliffe was pitching, and he was still a good veteran pitcher back then. He falls behind, 2-0, and then Junior starts fouling off some pitches, and then it's 3-2. Sutcliffe throws the next eight pitches in all sorts of spots, at all different speeds, and Griff is fouling them off. Sutcliffe is throwing him change-ups, spitters, curveballs, and he can't get the kid out. Finally, Sutcliffe throws him a fastball that's just a couple of inches out of the strike zone, and Junior takes it for a walk.

"That at-bat convinced me he was ready for the big leagues."

Looking back, Sutcliffe recalls, "I thought I was pitching to Willie Mays at the time. I guess I was."

In Junior's first major league at-bat, at Oakland's Alameda County Coliseum, he doubled on a pitch thrown by Dave Stewart. This was Dave Stewart at his prime, the Stewart who would win 21 games that year for his third consecutive 20-victory season.

Then came Ken's 18 consecutive at-bats without a hit, but surprisingly, Junior felt no panic or fear of being sent down. "I just tried not to worry about anything," he said. "You know what they say: You don't get too high and you don't get too low."

His first major league home run came off Chicago's Eric King April 10 at the Kingdome, the first time he'd set foot in his new home ballpark. Ironically, that date was his father's 39th birthday. When he called his dad to brag about his home run and how great it was that it came on his birthday, Griffey Sr. remarked, "You're not

getting away with my birthday that cheaply. Send me something."

Griffey's rookie season was pretty much a breeze. He went on to hit 16 homers, drive in 61 runs and hit .264 in 127 games. He missed 26 days from late July through Aug. 20 after breaking the middle knuckle of his right hand in an off-the-field injury that never really was explained. Otherwise, Griffey probably would have hit more than 20 homers and knocked in 90 runs.

From city to city, Griffey was the center of attention to the point that Lefebvre issued an edict that visiting writers could speak to Griffey only at a designated time before the first game of every series. Griffey was allowed to speak to reporters after games, too. "I wanted him to concentrate on playing baseball and developing. I didn't want him spending all his free time talking to the media. He was a teenager, and he needed

Although manager Jim Lefebvre knew that Griffey would be a player to watch, many stadiums remained empty when the Mariners came to town.

time to be a teenager," Lefebvre recalls.

In Seattle, where his arrival awakened a dead baseball city, Griffey lived by himself in an apartment near the ballpark. The Mariners had several veteran players and other former high draft picks on the team, but Griffey was so young it was hard for him to become chummy with anyone. He spent more time hanging around the batboys and Lefebvre's son, Ryan, that year because they were closest to him in age. Second baseman Harold Reynolds kept the closest watch over him, once quipping, "He can't get into trouble. He's on the phone all the time."

Junior thoroughly enjoyed himself that season. Though he was baseball savvy because of his early exposure to game, one scene early in the season caught him off guard.

During a game, the coaches motioned him to move over in the outfield, but he kept moving back to his original spot. When he got to the dugout, they asked him why he moved back. He explained that he couldn't see the batter because the second base umpire was blocking his view.

The coaches told him that he could ask the ump to move. "I didn't know that," he replied. The next night, huge Ken Kaiser was working second base, and Griffey asked him to move. Kaiser wouldn't budge. "We forgot to tell you," his teammates said. "Kaiser won't move for anybody, especially a 19-year-old rookie."

Then one time in May when the team was flying to Chicago, Lefebvre asked one of his coaches to send another message to Griffey. "Tell him to be at early batting practice at 3:30." Lefebvre recalls that not long after the message was delivered, Griffey came up to the front of the plane. Wearing a worried look, Junior asked, "What did I do wrong?"

"I assured him he had done nothing wrong," Lefebvre says. "This was interesting, though. By me telling him he should take early BP, he thought I was punishing him. He never had to do that before. He had been so successful wherever he'd been that early BP was a form of punishment to him."

The manager engaged the kid in a few closed-door conversations that year. People often criticized Griffey for dogging it, an action that infuriated Lefebvre.

"The one flaw he had was that when he hit a ball to second base, he would slow up after a while because he knew he was out," Lefebvre explains. "We changed that a little bit because everyone seemed to be looking for something to blame the kid with."

The Pacific Trading Card Company brought even more attention to the young phenom when it introduced a Ken Griffey Jr. chocolate bar. One Seattle columnist thought the best name for such a product would be Junior Mints, but the candy bar, which cost $1 and came in two attractive wrappers — one predominantly blue with gold accents and one predominantly gold with blue accents — was a big hit in the Great Northwest. One problem: Griffey was allergic to chocolate.

"I break out if I eat chocolate," he says.

He was the game's innocent child that year. He was too young to remember the 1975 World Series between the Reds and Red Sox. But he remembered his dad talking about the greatness of that postseason, something Junior said he wanted to experience before his career was done.

Ken Griffey Jr. finally experienced the drama and thrill of his own postseason appearance in 1995 when the Mariners defeated the Yankees in a classic five-game series. However, now that Griffey has tasted playoff success, he since has modified his goals to include playing in a World Series and even winning a championship someday. And with the confidence Griffey's possessed since Day One now beginning to spread, a World Series title in Seattle appears more credible heading into the 1996 season.

He emerged from his rookie season unscarred by the deluge of attention. His cap still wasn't on straight, but his head was. And that's all that mattered.   •

Nick Cafardo covers Major League Baseball for The Boston Globe *and is the author of an upcoming book on Atlanta pitcher Tom Glavine.*

Relaxing in the dugout was easy for the 19-year-old Griffey, already a veteran to the major league atmosphere.

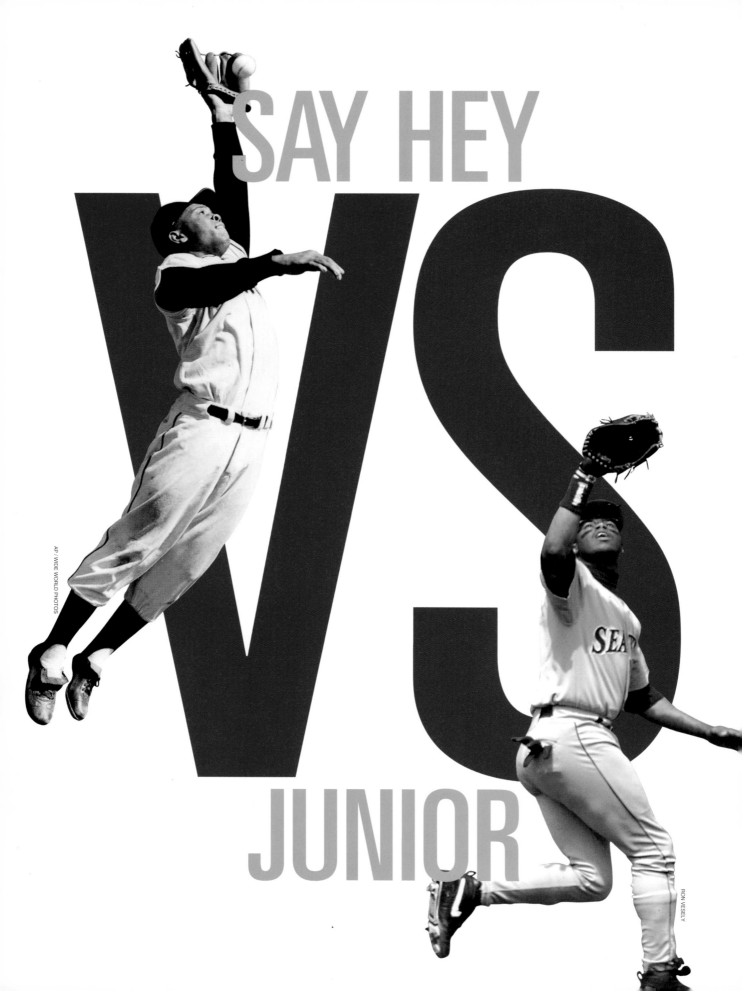

SAY HEY

VS

JUNIOR

Baseball analyst Tim McCarver lends his opinions for a comparison of Willie Mays and Ken Griffey Jr.

Since his first days as a major league player, Tim Mc-Carver has seen more than a generation of big-leaguers pass before his discerning eyes.

From two vantage points behind the plate — as a catcher for 21 years (and parts of four decades) and as an announcer for national baseball telecasts — Mc-Carver has watched one Griffey come and go and another become one of the game's elite.

We asked him to share his insights about Ken Griffey Jr. and the player to whom Junior is most often compared — Willie Mays.

I will say — and of course, I'm not alone in this — that Willie Mays is the best player I've ever seen, played with, played against, what-

By Tim McCarver (as told to Marty Noble)

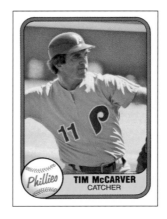

McCarver gained his baseball savvy behind the plate.

ever. I don't see how you could be any better than he was in every category.

However, Ken Griffey Jr. is the best young player I've ever seen, and I think it remains to be seen whether he will be talked about like Willie is today.

One would think that he will be.

To be talked about in the same breath as Willie Mays is an extraordinary accomplishment, regardless of your potential talent, regardless of how good you are at a certain age, that's high praise.

The most important quality Mays had as a player was his instincts. Nobody had instincts like this guy — to run the bases, to always be where the ball was.

Mays had that style, like with the basket catch, which always made me think that Mays never was in the proper position to throw. Throwing, to me, was one of the problems that he had.

I don't know that anybody ever exploited that because he charged the ball so well and he played shallow. You never had a chance to exploit it. I think players could have done that a little more with Willie.

I don't think you can do that with Junior. He's always in a position to throw.

If Willie had any dent in his armor, it was his throwing. I say that now, but I didn't say that as much then because he was Willie Mays. He intimidated you in every phase of the game.

Mays was a notorious off-speed hitter. It appears to me that Griffey has all the guile that Willie had at the plate, and maybe a greater ability to pull the ball.

It appears the way that Griffey rolls the top hand over, that he can pull the ball more naturally than Mays.

Maybe Willie, had he played at the Polo Grounds for his whole career, would have been a pull hitter.

I think Ken Griffey can

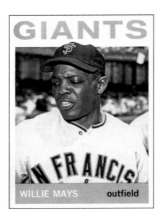

"Say Hey" Willie Mays inspired a generation.

hit 60 home runs. I really do. I think he's got a maturity about him that obviously was abetted by growing up around ballparks with his father.

It seems to be that the fun that he has is a real legitimate type of fun. He seems to be such an authentic young man.

It's kind of like Ripken being able to handle things

Junior's game is great and getting even better.

as well as he did. Part of that was because of his authenticity. He's real.

But I consider it a privilege to have played against Willie Mays. Even when he wasn't actually making a play, Mays was the kind of guy who made you say, "I'm going to watch him even when somebody else is hitting, even when he's on the field, even when he's moving around between pitches."

Of course, I wasn't as sophisticated a baseball fan then as I am now.   •

Marty Noble covers the Mets for New York Newsday.

PITCH

Way out, if you're smart. A ball in Ken Griffey Jr.'s wheel-house usually turns into a souvenir quicker than a pitcher can say . . . oops!

Dennis Martinez is a seasoned, solid pro. He's one of those stone-faced guys who rarely breaks his routine on the hill regardless of the hitter or the situation.

Yet there was Martinez in the first game of the American League Championship Series, messing with Ken Griffey Jr. like they were two kids playing stickball.

Griffey, in his first at-bat of the series, stepped into the batter's box, then out. In, out. In, out. Once he stepped out so late that Martinez had already started his delivery to the plate. When he saw umpire Davey Phillips raise his hands, he had to shut himself

By Phil Rogers

down in mid-motion. He glared at Griffey for a split second.

With Griffey then dug in for a pitch, Martinez wound up, started his delivery to the plate and finished it — all while still holding on to the ball. No balk was called, because no one was on base. Martinez was trying to crawl inside Griffey's head.

Who can blame him?

Conventional weapons such as fastballs, sliders and forkballs work only sporadically against Griffey. Why not try something unconventional?

"I wanted him to know I didn't like him stepping out," Martinez says. "I wanted him to see what it felt like. I also wanted to surprise him the next time, when I actually threw the ball."

Griffey eventually worked Martinez for a walk. It was no wonder Martinez didn't want to challenge the Mariners'

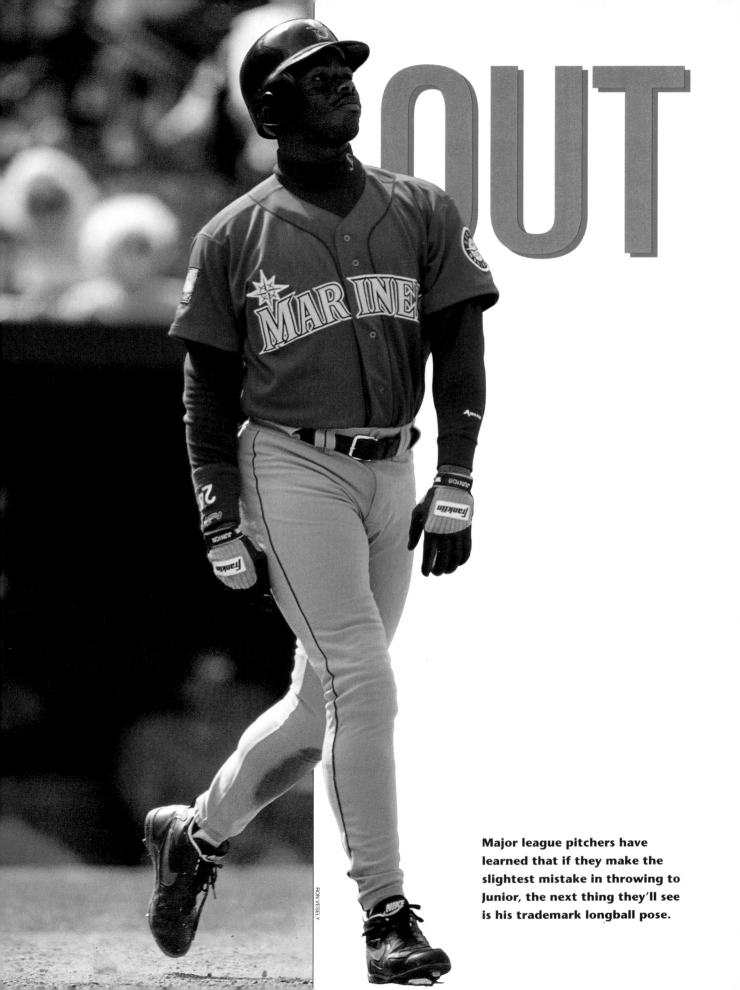

OUT

RON VESELY

Major league pitchers have learned that if they make the slightest mistake in throwing to Junior, the next thing they'll see is his trademark longball pose.

center fielder. Griffey needed just seven playoff games to tie the all-time record with six playoff homers. Give half the credit to American League batting champion Edgar Martinez, Griffey's protection in the four hole.

"If they batted anyone besides Edgar behind Junior, I don't believe he would ever see a pitch in the strike zone," a National League advance scout says. "Even with Edgar protecting him, I'm not so sure how smart it is to throw strikes to this guy. Does he ever look bad?"

Not often.

Not anymore.

Griffey Jr. arrived at The Show as a 19-year-old with enough raw skills to dominate for flashes. He now possesses the type of refinement that makes him dominate seasons. His skills as a hitter seem to improve every season. In turn, pitching to him becomes an increasingly difficult, make that impossible, proposition.

"When he first came up, I remember being amazed by his bat speed," veteran reliever Jeff Russell says. "But he wasn't the most patient hitter. You could get him out by keeping the ball out of the strike zone. I wish he was still chasing pitches."

Griffey hit .264 as a rookie in 1989, including a paltry .212 against lefthanders. It took him a year to adjust. He hit .300, with a .306 average against lefties, in 1990. He drove in 100 runs for the first time in 1991, batting .327. But the early success carried a price. He became so aggressive, it worked against him.

In 1992, Griffey hit the first pitch he saw 109 times in 617 plate appearances. He averaged just 3.41 pitches per plate appearance. For the first time in his career, his batting average declined. He "slumped" to .308.

Again, Griffey adjusted.

Griffey swung at the first pitch 91 times in '93, then 64 times in '94. It

has truly become the job of pitchers to get him out. He no longer plans to do it for them.

Griffey's broken left wrist was still bothering him in the postseason last year. He had never quite regained the flexibility he had before crashing into the Kingdome wall May 27. Griffey hit .255 with 10 homers and 27 RBI in 46 games after rushing back to the lineup in the heat of the pennant race.

"No one plan ever works on Junior, but here's the latest one," Toronto Blue Jays special assignment scout Gordon Lakey says. "Jam the daylights out of him. He's still a little vulnerable with his hand. You pitch him down and away and he can extend his arms and hurt you. But nothing he does amazes me. That ball he hit out [off New York's David Cone in the AL Division Series opener], he hit it with one hand on the bat. Do you believe that?"

Pitchers believe. They have seen Griffey do amazing things for years now. They know that any game plan must be perfectly executed . . . or else.

"The worst thing you can do — I mean, THE worst — is to try to go inside and not get the ball all the way in," Russell says. "If you go inside, you have to make sure you get the ball all the way in there. Once you've gone inside once or twice, then you have to be able to use your off-speed stuff."

Griffey's home run total dropped from 45 in 1993, his last full season, to 40 in the strike-shortened '94 season and 17 in '95, when he played just 72 games. No one around baseball expects it to stay down in '96. Griffey is too good at making adjustments according to both how he is being pitched and how he is swinging the bat.

Griffey arrived in the big leagues as a groundball hitter. In his first three seasons, Griffey hit 109

WORTH THE WAIT

Season	Pitches PPA	HRs PPA
1989	3.51	1:31.6
1990	3.59	1:30.3
1991	3.53	1:28.4
1992	3.41	1:22.3
1993	3.57	1:15.4
1994	3.63	1:12.3
1995	3.83	1:18.5

After six seasons of worrying and planning, major league pitchers have arrived at one simple way to keep Junior from going deep every time up: Break his bat.

TOM DIPACE

After his hastened recovery from a broken wrist, Junior's lone weakness at the end of the '95 season was the perfectly placed inside pitch.

more grounders than flies (567-458). In his last three seasons, he has hit 89 more fly balls than grounders (450-361).

"For a hitter to make that transition, which he makes trying to utilize his power, and remain a high-average hitter is truly amazing," Seattle hitting coach Lee Elia says. "What it tells you is he's doing just the thing you always tell kids not to do — swing for the fences — and, in his case, it is the right thing to do."

Griffey sees power as only another part of his all-around approach as a hitter. "If the home runs help us win, fine," he says. "But they don't mean any more than anything else anyone does on our team to help out. Like the homer I hit [in the eighth inning of Game 5 against New York]. I liked my single in the 11th more because it was part of the winning rally."

Danny Darwin predicted Griffey's game-winning hit off Texas lefty Dennis Cook on Sept. 17. With the winning run on second in the 11th inning, Griffey put an inside-out swing on a fastball, lining the game-winning hit off third baseman Luis Ortiz's glove.

"I had just said, 'He's going to try to hit the ball to left,' " Darwin recalls. "Then he did it. He's probably the best hitter I've seen in the clutch. He's got everything you look for."

Griffey seems to become more disciplined at the plate with each birthday. He waits for just the right pitch, in just the right zone. He saw 3.83 pitches per plate appearance in 1995, the most of his career. He swung at the first pitch just 38 times.

"He's got a good eye, great hand-eye coordination," Russell notes. "He's like a Wade Boggs, except with power."

No wonder Martinez didn't want to throw the ball.

Who would?   •

Phil Rogers is a sportswriter for The Dallas Morning News.

TOTAL RECALL

Never one to forget a nasty pitch, Griffey Jr. rarely gets fooled twice

Ken Griffey Jr. doesn't keep a book on pitchers. He doesn't need one. He has all the information he needs stored away in his own personal database.

"Guys get me out, I'm going to remember them," Griffey says. "I don't know why. I don't know how. I just remember things, especially when guys get me out."

Hitting coach Lee Elia, who has been with Seattle since 1993, says he has worked with few hitters with a memory like Griffey's. "There was one," Elia says. "I shouldn't name names, but it was Pete Rose."

Unlike some of the game's premier batsmen such as Tony Gwynn, Griffey seldom studies videos of opposing pitchers. He will glance at the videos that are played on clubhouse televisions before games, but it is more like a housewife watching a soap opera than a critic reviewing a movie. The important footage is filed away in Griffey's mind, where it has been since the last time he saw the pitcher.

"We're playing one game and this rookie pitcher is coming in from the bullpen," Elia says. "He's just been called up, and we don't have a scouting report on him. Nobody knows him. Then Junior says, 'Wait a minute, that's the guy who worked against us two years ago in spring training. He didn't throw me nothing but breaking balls. He's afraid to throw his fastball. Get ahead in the count, then he's got to come in to you.' He was exactly right."

Pitchers fear Griffey's total recall. It is so vivid, opponents can't follow any set pitching pattern when facing him.

"When you find something that works against him, you better not try it a second time," Toronto Blue Jays special assignment scout Gordon Lakey says. "If it worked once, it is not going to work again. You are asking for trouble when you try the same thing twice."

Griffey seldom worries about repeating himself. His mechanics are near flawless and he seems to take batting practice for pleasure rather than for work.

"With Junior, timing is everything," Elia explains. "He just goes out and takes his hacks, gets a feel for his timing that particular day. Nothing fancy."

When Griffey gets out of whack, he will bounce ideas off close friend Jay Buhner. They have played together since 1989.

"He's so mentally strong," Buhner says. "He believes — really and truly — he can do anything."

No one is arguing.
                                    — Phil Rogers

Memory

Junior never forgets a foe. He can remember a pitcher's strengths and weaknesses without studying any films or reports — even if he hasn't seen that pitcher in years.

Strength

He doesn't have the bulk of Frank Thomas or the girth of Cecil Fielder, but Junior still knows how to drive the ball into the bleachers. What he lacks in chest size, he makes up for with arm strength and bat speed.

Vision

Since the 1989 season, Junior has started looking for his pitch a little more closely. In that time, his plate appearances have lengthened on the average from 3.51 pitches to 3.83 pitches.

Hands

Junior's swing is the sweetest in the sport. He rolls his wrists so effortlessly that pulling the ball is easy. Yet he still has enough power to take the ball to the opposite field if he feels so inclined. His one weakness in late '95 was inside pitching aimed to exploit his healing left wrist.

Batter's Blueprint

From head to toe, Ken Griffey Jr. is a pitcher's nightmare

Legs

Junior pulls the ball or takes it the other way with pure upper-body strength, so he doesn't open or close his stance very often. His speed is such that a single can easily become a double if the outfield isn't paying attention.

Not only has Ken Griffey Jr.

become a favorite among baseball

fans nationwide, he's also

become an irresistible

subject for all types

of artists. His humble and

milesofsmiles

happy-go-lucky demeanor

off the field complements

his consistent brilliance

on the field, thus making

The Kid worthy of the

following artistic tribute.

leslie woods

KEN GRIFFEY JR.

murray tinkelman

tim cortes

KEN GRIFFEY JR.

amy chenier

ed gragg

anthony douglas

KEN GRIFFEY JR.

fred dingler

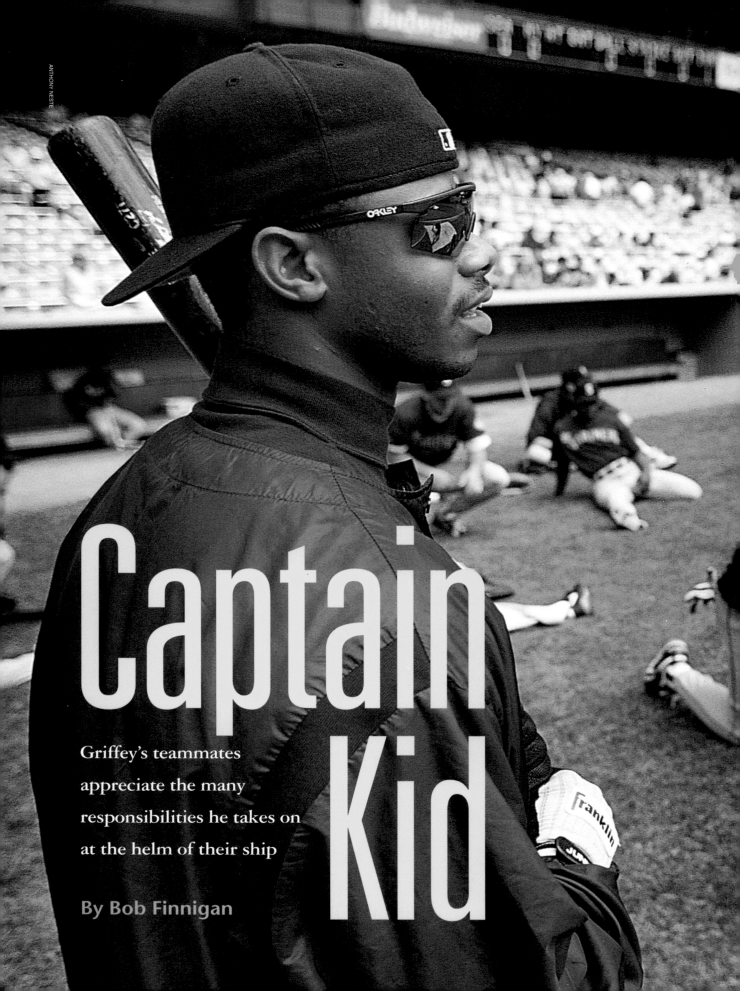

Captain Kid

Griffey's teammates appreciate the many responsibilities he takes on at the helm of their ship

By Bob Finnigan

Not long after 26-year-old outfielder Eric Anthony joined the Seattle Mariners in 1994, at spring training in Arizona he joined veterans Jay Buhner and Ken Griffey Jr. at a card table amidst the hubbub of the crowded clubhouse almost every day to share lunch.

Inviting Anthony was Griffey's idea. It was his way of quickly making a new teammate part of the club, of solidifying what everyone hoped would be a tight outfield unit for many seasons to come.

The hoped-for union did not reach expectations. Unable to cope with the American League's off-speed pitching, Anthony was gone a year later, another in a series of 30-something different left fielders Griffey and Buhner have played with in a half-dozen seasons.

But the experience, and the impressions formed, stuck with Anthony. "Before I got to Seattle, I had heard stories about Junior's ego getting in his way," says Anthony, who wound up playing well for Cincinnati a year later. "Ken does have an ego, but if he thinks he's better than anyone else it's only as a player. . . . And he is a better player than anyone else. And on the Seattle club, in that clubhouse, he never shows that. And he certainly doesn't hold himself above anyone as a person.

"Believe it or not, I think Junior would like nothing better than to be regarded as just another one of the guys. It's everyone around him who won't let him. He's a great guy as well as a great player."

There's no doubt that Griffey receives considerations afforded no one else on the Mariners. But there probably never has been a team on which the franchise player does not get — or rate — special attention.

Certain Seattle club officials, for instance, often speak to him about the direction they are taking the team, regarding playing matters from personnel or marketing to the recent, successful civic campaign to win local government approval to build a ballpark. "We don't defer to Junior, and it's nothing like asking permission or even his opinion," one club official says. "But he's interested in what's going on. He's got a good mind and a good feel for the team and the fans. If you have a franchise player like him, it makes sense he is involved to a degree."

Griffey speaks his mind often on issues involving the franchise, but only once has he taken a firm public stance on personnel matters. That came in the winter of 1994-95, when it appeared that Buhner, his close friend and outfield mate, could sign as a free agent with the Baltimore Orioles. Junior ripped the front office over the possibility of losing Buhner. "If Jay goes, they better get ready to send me someplace else, too," he said. "The front office talks about not being able to make a better offer. They call it business. Well, I call it bull———."

Buhner was re-signed. "I can't tell you how much I appreciate Junior going to bat for me like that," Buhner later said. "I never wanted to leave Seattle."

When it comes to creating commotion in the clubhouse, Griffey is a one-man racket. From the comfort of his vibrating easy chair in his corner locker, he constantly jokes, critiques or insults anyone in the room, often from some distance away, usually at multidecibel levels. The young assistants to clubhouse manager Henry Genzale are both his targets and his pals. When he gets up from his chair, it's usually for pregame workouts, the game itself, or to engage one of them in the video game he installed in the weight room.

With their superstar back in the lineup, the Mariners had plenty of reasons to celebrate during their first-ever postseason playoff appearance last year.

"He's fun," says Michael Spears, who has worked in the clubhouse for 15 years. "He likes you to do a lot for him, but he takes care of us, too."

Whenever Griffey is looking for a piece of equipment, he typically hollers, "Hen-ree!!!!" and Genzale comes over to help.

When Griffey missed three months of the 1995 season after fracturing his left wrist, pitcher Chris Bosio looked puzzled the second day Junior was gone. "It's so quiet here in the clubhouse," he said. "We're going to miss Griff on the field, but I think we may miss his act in here almost as much. He keeps everyone on their toes. It often seems like the bigger a game we face, the noisier he gets . . . as if he's telling everyone to relax."

Outside of Clan Griffey, no one can offer better insight into Junior's impact on the team than Buhner. "A lot of us like to think we do some leading on this team," he says. "I try some. Unit [pitcher Randy Johnson] definitely does. But Ken is The Man on the Mariners.

"Everyone sees the money he gets and the performances he's expected to give — and usually does — to earn it. But there's so much more that goes into what he does both to earn his money and to help our team. This last season, especially in the postseason, we all got a lot of media attention, but day-in, day-out, the press hovers around Kenny. And he deals with it."

Indeed, when Griffey speaks, as is the case with the leader on any club, people listen. The media typically gather around, ask a question or two and let Junior do what he loves to — talk to people. Buhner compared him to Reggie Jackson or Dave Winfield taking much of the heat from Yankees owner George Steinbrenner and from New York fans.

Griffey's enthusiasm and loose style of play on the field carries over to his teammates in the dugout and in the clubhouse.

As longtime teammates who have spent the majority of their baseball careers together, Jay Buhner and Griffey have become close friends.

"Junior does that for us. He talks and lets the rest of us go about our business, preparing for games or playing them," Buhner says. "He leaves a group of reporters or visitors in the clubhouse — he always spends as much time as he can with kids who come in, definitely any handicapped kids — goes and picks up his glove and starts the game. And the numbers show how he plays. He runs one-man interference for us then goes out and out-plays everyone."

That's not to say there aren't any rubs. Reigning AL Cy Young winner Randy Johnson's personality is the opposite of Griffey's: dour, gloomy, especially on days when he starts. Johnson's humor is more whimsical and less frequent than Griffey's — which could be said for almost everyone else on the team. As typically happens with two superior performers on the same club, the two get along but are not close. "I think we share a mutual respect, and that's what counts," Johnson says. "We each help the team in our own ways."

Ironically, while Johnson does not need much offensive support in most games, Griffey seems to excel in an exceptional number of his starts. For instance, Junior hit the three-run homer that made Johnson a winner on Opening Day last season, and in Johnson's victory over Baltimore on May 26, Griffey homered early then helped kill fifth-inning trouble with a crashing catch that broke his wrist. Johnson paid homage to the effort with a fake faint of disbelief on the mound — before realizing his teammate was injured.

"I appreciate what Junior does for me and the other pitchers," Johnson says. "Sometimes, a lot of things others do get overlooked because Junior is so good."

Griffey's support for his teammates takes other forms. Two years ago, he offered to restructure his multiyear contract to help the Mariners sign free agents. Last year, he offered to do it again. "He offered to defer the money, at no interest, against my judgment," agent Brian Goldberg says. "He's made the offer several times.

"I think we all know most of the things Junior does for the team, but I imagine there's a lot we don't ever hear about," former teammate Tino Martinez says. "He's an amazing player and an amazing person. He was just fun to be around. He shared himself. I'm going to miss him."

When Ken returned to the lineup from his broken wrist last Aug. 15, he jokingly reintroduced himself to his teammates, as "George" — his real first name. Shortly thereafter, he needed help finding something. The familiar yell — "Hen-ree!!!" — reverberated throughout the clubhouse. "That," Genzale, "is music to my ears."   •

Bob Finnigan covers the Mariners for The Seattle Times.

Youth

Ken Griffey Jr.'s endearing appeal to kids makes him as good at delivering a pitch as he is at smashing one out of the park

By Bob Finnigan

is Served

The kids knew before anyone. They knew what Ken Griffey Jr. would someday become.

In the spring of 1989, before Griffey's fame and fortune made security a priority, young fans waited for the Mariners' outfield prospect in the lobby of the team hotel in Tempe, Ariz., and a half-dozen or so hung around the hallway near his room every evening.

Griffey came out every night and chatted with them — just one of the quiet group, just kids in the hall. About what? "Just stuff," replied one of the kids, a boy about 14 years old.

Griffey's take was no different: "Just stuff."

Junior was almost the same age as those who came to him in admiration. In his first big-league camp, Griffey was a lonely kid himself. This was no publicity thing, no hype. This was the first and maybe the purest example of the affinity kids have with Griffey.

"The kids just love him because he enjoys what he does as much as he is good at it," says Lauren Pierce, mother of three children who sought Griffey's autograph after a spring practice. "He's so positive, and it seems like he smiles all the time. Parents love him because you feel you can trust him. There's no scandal, no playboy stuff, just a good guy and a good player."

But Griffey isn't The Kid anymore. After the birth of his first child, son Trey, in January 1994, Griffey asked the media to stop using the moniker he had worn so gracefully since he was a teenage phenom swinging his way into The Show.

What has remained, though, is the bond between Ken Griffey Jr. and his fans. As that group in the hall expanded to a generation across the country, the Mariners' star center fielder didn't lose touch with his followers — especially the young ones.

He has kept that kinship alive with dazzling play and sheer personality, the big Griffey grin and basic good nature.

That superstar/entertainer quality also has made Griffey a marketing success away from the ballpark. An intentionally small portfolio of commercials and endorsements provides what *Forbes* magazine recently estimated between $1.5 million and $2 million beyond the $7 million he makes with the Mariners.

"We try to be careful in what we do," says Brian Goldberg, Junior's Cincinnati-based agent. "First of all, there is the matter of time. Ken simply couldn't do all he is asked to take part in. But probably more important to Ken is taste."

That's not taste as in All-Sport, the energy drink Griffey pitches in television commercials. Goldberg is referring to suitability for Griffey's audience of families and young fans.

Nike is Griffey's main endorsement outlet. The Oregon-based company has made Junior one of its leading figures.

"Baseball players don't have the appeal for Nike that basketball and football players do," Goldberg says. "But they have treated Ken really well. You could say we're into phase two of the relationship."

"Phase two" means that like Nintendo, which renewed Griffey as a spokesman after Sega expressed interest in him, Nike is into its

Junior On-Line

If you're a fan of Ken Griffey Jr. and a frequent passenger on the information superhighway, you'll find your fix of The Kid at:

http://www.mariners.org/ken.jr/ken.jr.home.html

And if you're looking for Junior's fan club in cyberspace, you'll want to go to:

http://www.mariners.org/ken.jr/inside.ticket/inside.ticket.html

Of course, for those fans who prefer the old-fashioned mail, the address is:

**Sports Fan Network
Ken Griffey Jr.'s Inside Ticket
Attn: Internet
P.O. Box 581
Portland, OR 97207-0581**

second contractual arrangement with Griffey.

Griffey also was the centerpiece of an advertising campaign that featured last year's commercial in which he chased a Don Mattingly fly ball out of Yankee Stadium and across the country, only to make a diving catch on a California beach before making a throw to nip a runner at home back in New York.

Griffey also has designed several athletic shoes for Nike. One — Air Diamond Fury — hit the market last year and another is soon to be introduced. At Griffey's insistence, the price of the shoe is kept below the $100-plus some endorsed brands cost.

"These are for kids to wear," he says, "not put in a frame."

Lynn Merritt, who works for Nike and with Griffey, says Junior's connection with Nike is "big and soon to get bigger — as big as our association with Michael Jordan. Junior is going to be one of our brand leaders, a superstar of the 1990s into the 2000s.

"We think Junior's got it all. His athletic skills are tremendous; he's like the Jordan of baseball. He's got personality — fresh, clean and vibrant. He's just a tremendous guy and we think all that comes across in the commercials."

Nike's next step is the release of Air Griffey II. The new commercial campaign should be the company's biggest since "Bo Knows," which made Bo Jackson more than a two-sport hero about five years ago.

In a television spot for Nike, Griffey aired himself out after a cross-country dash to catch a fly ball.

KEN GRIFFEY JR.

Griffey's ties to the Northwest are not limited to Nike, however. Griffey's renewal with Nintendo, based in the Seattle area, was based not so much on money as it was on loyalty.

"Ken could have played that out some," Goldberg says. "Sega was very interested. But there were strong ties to Nintendo — Northwest-based — and with their part in the Mariners team ownership."

Nintendo of America, the North American arm of the huge Japanese company, is the majority owner of the Seattle baseball team.

"What was also important," Griffey adds, "is that I wanted more input in the design and development of my baseball game. When Nintendo said that was all right, the deal was done. I like helping come up with things to make the game more realistic."

While Griffey's sweet swing took Seattle by storm in his rookie season, The Kid indulged his sweet tooth with the release of Ken Griffey Jr. chocolate bars. Fans, in turn, gobbled up more than a million of them.

Upper Deck has realized Junior's broad appeal as well, using Griffey's image in ads for its baseball cards. Even Major League Baseball is riding on Ken's bandwagon, using the sport's most magnetic personality in a campaign to win fans back after the strike of '94.

But away from the field, Griffey is more than just a poster boy with a glowing grin. Junior's creative side has taken root in acting, including using his voice for a cartoon character of himself on an episode of *The Simpsons.*

He also played himself in the 1994 comedy *Little Big League,* a Castle Rock Entertainment film in which a 12-year-old becomes the manager/owner of the Minnesota Twins.

"In all his work so far," Goldberg explains, "Ken has played himself, on *Medicine Ball* and the time he was on *Harry and the Hendersons* along with his dad. What he really wants to do is play someone other than himself."

In other words, Griffey's dream is to play a bad guy.

"I'd love to be a drug dealer in a cop show," he says. "It's something wild, something way out of character. Then I could pay for it at

AP / WIDE WORLD PHOTOS

the end, get shot, do a nasty fall and die."

He was scheduled to do episodes for *New York Undercover,* playing a young partner to a veteran cop, and for *Lois & Clark* last spring, but a more exciting option presented itself.

"Then they settled the strike," he says. "No more acting. I was just happy to get back playing ball."

Last winter, he studied several movie scripts for possible role offers but didn't have the time to read them. He's also dabbled in music, working on songs with M.C. Hammer.

"The acting and the music have helped give me an idea of what I want to do with my life after baseball," Griffey says. "But I know that right now I have to do well in baseball for anything else to happen. You can't let anything affect your playing, and if you play well, they'll keep asking you to do shows and design games and shoes . . . and have fun."

Having fun is what being a kid is all about. And despite ditching the tag, the player formerly known as The Kid continues to have the most fun of all.　　　　　　　　　　　•

Bob Finnigan covers the Mariners for The Seattle Times.

Fans fear not -- the larger-than-life Griffey has not turned to endorsing alcoholic beverages. Instead, he has reinforced his "kid-at-heart" appeal by renewing his agreement with Nintendo.

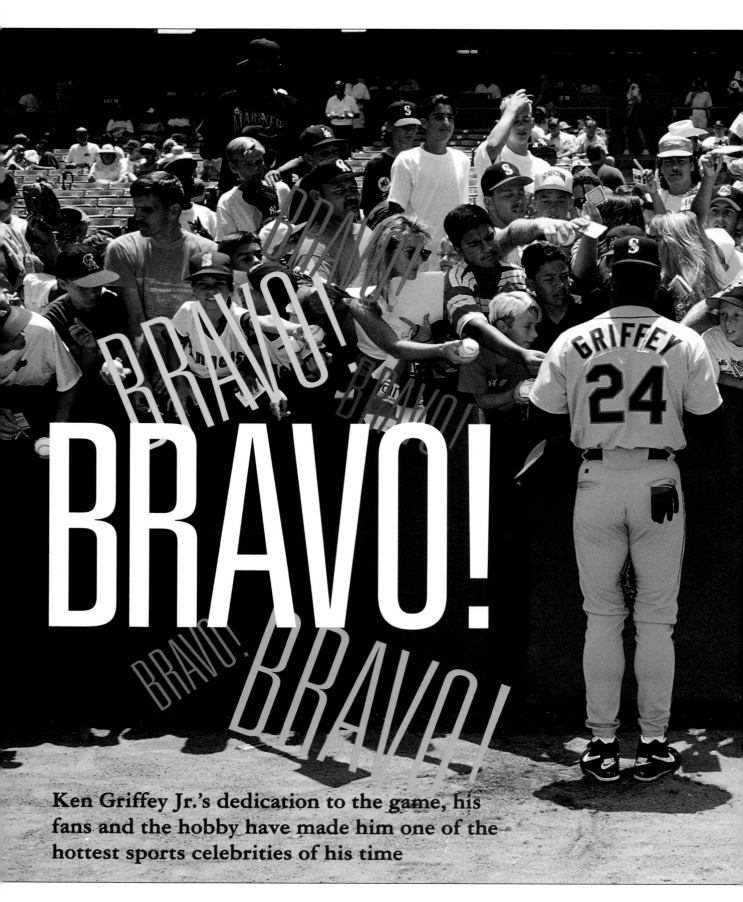

BRAVO!
BRAVO! BRAVO! BRAVO! BRAVO! BRAVO! BRAVO! BRAVO!

Ken Griffey Jr.'s dedication to the game, his fans and the hobby have made him one of the hottest sports celebrities of his time

MITCHELL HADDAD

By Grant Sandground

I f you're planning to add every Ken Griffey Jr. card to your collection, you'd better sit down. Maybe you should reconsider going after everything. This Griffey collecting business can get messy.

For one thing, Junior has more than 700 cards to his name. That's 700 and counting. And if you're still bent on gathering all things Junior, you'd better check the balance on your savings account. You'll need more than $6,000 to get one of each of his issues.

On the next few pages, we offer a year-by-year look at Junior's brief but most successful history in the hobby.

1989

After the Seattle Mariners made him the No. 1 overall pick in the 1987 draft, Ken Griffey Jr. wasted no time in becoming a hobby hero. He ran neck-and-neck with fellow newcomers Gary Sheffield and Gregg Jefferies in the popularity race in the summer of '89, but by season's end, Griffey was in a league of his own.

Best Card

1989 Upper Deck #1. The '89 Upper Deck set was a hit with collectors from the start, offering the highest quality card to date. This card still stands as one of the most significant baseball cards issued in the last 20 years — possibly ever.

Toughest Card

1989 Donruss Rookies #3. This issue may be pretty tough to find, considering it was a hobby-only factory set issue.

Coolest Card

1989 Upper Deck #1. No comments are needed — this is the card.

Unfortunate Issue

1989 Bowman #259. Collectors are well aware how significant the Griffey father-son tandem has been, but this card didn't do either Griffey justice.

Coolest Card

1990 Leaf #245. Like the Upper Deck issued a year before, Leaf's card of Junior broke new ground in the hobby.

Unfortunate Issue

1990 Upper Deck #24 Team Checklist. Vernon Wells' art is commendable, but the background and design of the card front are somewhat lackluster.

1990

Griffey's sophomore season was surprisingly quiet in the hobby. His '89 Upper Deck Rookie Card actually dipped from $10 to $9 early that year before shooting up to $30 by December.

Best Card

1990 Leaf #245. This issue seems like an anomaly in that every player (except Griffey) who has a 1989 Upper Deck Rookie Card has a 1990 Leaf card that's similar in value. However, Griffey's '89 Upper Deck issue is the anomaly here, since its value is so high. The '90 Leaf set took the hobby by storm, ushering in a second wave of production quality, coupled with perceived scarcity.

Toughest Card

1990 Fleer Soaring Stars #6. Issued randomly in 1990 Fleer jumbo packs only, cards from the 12-card Soaring Stars set were overlooked by collectors when they were first issued. They enjoyed a modest comeback in 1994 as collectors started searching for more remotely distributed insert cards.

1991

Junior moved to the front of the baseball card market, establishing himself as one of the sport's most dominating players. Virtually all of his cards were in heavy demand — particularly his '89 Upper Deck RC, which jumped in value by about 600 percent from early '90 to the end of '91.

Best Card

1991 Stadium Club #270. The '91 Stadium Club set challenged collectors' ideas of how far premium quality could be taken in a baseball card. With Griffey's surging popularity, this card was naturally a hot item with its release.

Toughest Card

1991 Score Cooperstown #B3. Because 1991 was the peak of the overproduction era, no Griffey cards from that year are truly difficult to find. Still, the Cooperstown cards are the most obscure from that year, issued in complete set form in the '91 Score factory sets only.

Coolest Card

1991 Score #892 Dream Team. This card features a great design and a crisp, clean studio photo in black and white. The card also captures a slice of history: Junior somehow looks even younger than he was at the time.

Unfortunate Issue

1991 Score #841. Everything right about the black-and-white Griffey issue #892 is wrong when it come to this card. Good idea, not-so-good execution.

Unfortunate Issue

1992 Triple Play #152. A blurry photo doesn't help his card, and the fact that Junior's not holding the bat, which is making contact with the ball, serves only as a means to a confusing end.

1992

Griffey's hobby status became official: The Kid turned into The Man. As Junior became one of the sport's premier players, he soared to the top of collectors' charts as well.

Best Card

1992 Fleer Team Leaders #15. Cards from this set enjoyed a resurgence in popularity because of the stir initially created in Fleer's basketball and football Team Leaders sets. Though not as scarce as the pack-distributed basketball and football versions, the baseball Team Leaders still jumped in value by almost 300 percent at the peak of their popularity in 1994.

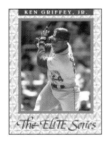

Toughest Card

1992 Donruss Elite #13. Today, a numbered print run of 10,000 cards doesn't seem that scarce, but back in '92, the run was microscopic. Elites are still printed in the same quantities today, but the case production numbers from 1992 to 1995 have reduced drastically. Thus, finding a '92 Griffey Elite is akin to finding a small island in the Pacific, while pulling a '95 Griffey Elite is like finding a rubber duck in a bathtub.

Coolest Card

1992 Pinnacle Slugfest #7. The dramatic, horizontally designed 15-card set caused a stir with its sharp design and retail-only distribution.

1993

The number of sets soared in '93, while production runs dwindled dramatically. The hobby experienced the first true cutback in growth in more than a decade, and card manufacturers responded by printing fewer cards in more sets. Griffey was his usual superstar self on the field, and his standing in the hobby remained intact.

Best Card

1993 Finest Refractor #110. This one's a no-brainer. Just 241 of these cards were produced, and they're worth almost $1,000 each. Really.

Toughest Card

1993 Finest Refractor #110. What else did you expect to see here?

Coolest Card

1993 SP Platinum Power #PP9. The hobby's first die-cut designed set is growing in significance each day as die-cut issues are gaining more and more in popularity. Upper Deck's debut SP product took a little time to be discovered because it was overshadowed by Finest in '93. The Griffey card represents the best card you can pull from a pack, and that is extremely cool.

Unfortunate Issue

1993 Score #504 All-Star. This card is not only the most unfortunate issue of '93, but it ranks pretty high on the all-time list as well. The cartoon image looks more like Jimmie "Dyno-Mite!" Walker than Ken Griffey Jr.

1994

The number of products remained stable, but the number of insert sets within each product grew. The result was about 125 new cards of Junior on the market.

Best Card

1994 SP Holoview Red #12. Possibly Junior's most desirable mainstream card, the scarce Holoview Reds were inserted at a rate of about one per 75 packs. Given that the set contains 40 cards, only one pack in 3,000 contains a Griffey Holoview Red.

Toughest Card

1994 Upper Deck Ken Griffey Jr./Mickey Mantle Autograph #GM. Griffey numbered and signed exactly 1,000 of these cards, which were inserted exclusively in Series I retail packs. Very tough to find.

Coolest Card

1994 Flair Hot Glove #3. This card is sharp, with a bold design for each of the 10 cards in the set. Hot Gloves were randomly inserted — one per 24 packs — in Flair Series II, a product printed only to order because of the strike.

Unfortunate Issue

1994 Sportflics #181 Starflics. This card features a shot of Junior bailing out on an off-speed pitch and also manages to feature two fuzzy baseballs.

The number of products and sets seemed to stabilize in '95, but the amount of money collectors had to pay for each card kept creeping upward, as did suggested retail pack prices and wholesale case prices.

Best Card

1995 Finest Refractor #118. By far the hottest insert set from the last season, the Griffey single from this scarce set (1:12 packs) is arguably the most desirable card in the set. In fact, it's right near the top of the list of the most desirable cards issued in 1995.

Toughest Card

1995 Select Artist's Proofs #89. The announced case run of 4,950 sent savvy hobbyists scurrying for their pocket calculators. The numbers revealed that just 475 Select Artist's Proofs were printed, resulting in a steady surge of demand that finally leveled off late in the year. (*Editor's note: Artist's Proof version not available for picturing*)

Coolest Card

1995 Pinnacle #128. You've got to love the look on Junior's face as he tries to keep his mammoth bubble from popping.

Unfortunate Issue

1995 Donruss Dominators #8. You can't fault the player selection on this insert card, but the design is cluttered, and the photos are sliced strangely. Also, should you peel the protective film or leave it on? Tough call. •

Grant Sandground is the assistant manager of pricing analysis for Beckett Publications.

SIGNATURE SUCCESS

Ken Griffey's Jr.'s overwhelming popularity and flare for the game has led to him becoming baseball's hottest commodity in the autographed memorabilia market

Ken Griffey Jr.'s status as the premier young superstar in baseball cannot be justified with statistics alone.

Mere numbers cannot begin to illustrate his charisma, his style, his flair for the dramatic, all of which make him so appealing.

Griffey's nicknames, "Junior" and "The Kid" offer some insight to his image as a tremendously gifted player who truly enjoys playing baseball. This image was what Nike and Upper Deck, among others, sought to portray when they chose him as an endorser.

Junior's standing as perhaps the best all-around player in the American League has only been enhanced by his sparkling off-field image. While he has had to take the normal precautions that go along with being one of the most famous athletes in America, he's still rightfully seen as one of the most fan-friendly superstars in the sport.

Griffey signs autographs at the park on a fairly regular basis. Some fans may recall a scene from spring training last year when Griffey instructed TV crews to turn off their cameras, then proceeded to sign for just about everyone in the stadium. His message: His feeling for the fans is genuine and sincere, not for show.

For collectors who don't have a chance to see Griffey in person very often, a variety of signed items is available in the open marketplace.

A ceramic plate personally autographed by Griffey can be obtained for as little as $30.

Autographed cards sell for about $15-$30, 8-by-10 color photos for about $20-$40. Single-signed official baseballs will cost collectors about $30-$50 (slightly more for All-Star balls), and unused bats sell anywhere from $125 to $200 depending on the model. For the ultimate Griffey collector, a signed game-model jersey can be obtained for about $250-$350.

Of course, as with any superstar, fake autographs are a big problem. Unless you are familiar with Griffey's John Hancock, you might want to stick with some cards and items issued by known reliable sources:

• Classic/Scoreboard had an agreement with Griffey during the early '90s, resulting in several items sold primarily through home shopping channels. Such items included special cards, plaques and single-signed baseballs. Griffey signed 3,100 individually numbered special cards that were randomly inserted in 1992 Classic/Best minor league packs. These cards list in *Beckett Future Stars* for $125-$200 each.

• Upper Deck inked Griffey as a spokesman prior to 1994. The 1994 Upper Deck Series I retail packs included randomly inserted 1,000 each autographed cards of Griffey (listed in *Beckett Baseball Card Monthly* for $150-$250), Mickey Mantle ($400-$600) and a Griffey/Mantle combo card ($700-$1000). In early 1996, UD issued Griffey autographed cards as bonuses to hobby dealers who ordered cases of 1996 Collector's Choice. Market value of these autographed issues was unknown at press time.

• And for those collectors who are seeking Griffey memorabilia for their china cabinets, Gartlan, a producer of limited edition ceramic sports collectibles, released an artwork plate personally signed with a gold-paint pen. Some closeouts have hit the market, resulting in a current market price of about $30-$50.

Although Griffey's splendid statistics may vary from season to season, one issue with The Kid always seems to remain a constant — his classy style and his genuine respect for baseball fans everywhere.

– Theo Chen

KEN GRIFFEY JR.'S COMPREHENSIVE CARD CHECKLIST & PRICE GUIDE

❑ '87 Bellingham Mariners
    team set (34)   75.00
❑ '88 Best San Bernardino Spirit
    team set (28)   90.00
❑ '88 Best San Bernardino Spirit
    team set Platinum (28)   300.00
❑ '88 Cal League All-Stars
    team set (50)   16.00
❑ '88 Cal League San Bernardino
    Spirit team set (28)   16.00
❑ '88 ProCards Vermont Mariners
    bonus card   25.00
❑ '89 Bowman #220   5.00
❑ '89 Bowman #259
    w/ Ken Griffey Sr.   1.00
❑ '89 Bowman Tiffany #220   30.00
❑ '89 Bowman Tiffany #259
    w/ Ken Griffey Sr.   6.00
❑ '89 Classic Travel Orange #131   9.00
❑ '89 Classic Travel Purple #193   4.00
❑ '89 Donruss #33   5.00
❑ '89 Donruss Baseball's Best #192   4.00
❑ '89 Donruss Rookies #3   5.00
❑ '89 Fleer #548   5.00
❑ '89 Fleer Glossy #548   20.00
❑ '89 Mariners Mother's #3   10.00
❑ '89 Mother's Griffey Jr. set (4)   15.00
❑ '89 Score Rookie/Traded #100T   5.00
❑ '89 Score Scoremasters #30   2.50
❑ '89 Score Young Superstars II #18   3.00
❑ '89 Topps Traded #41T   4.00
❑ '89 Topps Traded Tiffany #41T   20.00
❑ '89 Upper Deck #1   75.00
❑ '90 All-American Baseball
    Team #17   5.00
❑ '90 Bazooka #18   3.00
❑ '90 Bowman #481   2.00
❑ '90 Bowman Tiffany #481   20.00
❑ '90 Classic Blue #20   2.50
❑ '90 Classic Yellow #T1   2.00
❑ '90 Donruss #4 Diamond King   1.00
❑ '90 Donruss #365   2.00
❑ '90 Donruss Best AL #1   3.50
❑ '90 Donruss Learning Series #8   6.00
❑ '90 Donruss Super DKs #4   6.00
❑ '90 Fleer #513   2.00
❑ '90 Fleer Award Winners #16   1.25
❑ '90 Fleer Baseball All-Stars #14   1.25
❑ '90 Fleer Baseball MVP's #14   1.25
❑ '90 Fleer Canadian #513   6.00
❑ '90 Fleer League Leaders #14   1.25
❑ '90 Fleer Soaring Stars #6   20.00
❑ '90 Fleer Wax Box Cards #C10   2.50
❑ '90 Leaf #245   30.00
❑ '90 Leaf Previews #4   250.00
❑ '90 Mariners Mother's #3   5.00
❑ '90 O-Pee-Chee #336   1.50

'89 Upper Deck #1

❑ '90 Post #23   4.00
❑ '90 Score #560   2.00
❑ '90 Score 100 Rising Stars #3   2.00
❑ '90 Sportflics #7   7.00
❑ '90 Sunflower Seeds #2   4.00
❑ '90 Topps #336   2.00
❑ '90 Topps Big #250   5.00
❑ '90 Topps Debut '89 #46   5.00
❑ '90 Topps Glossy Send-Ins #20   2.00
❑ '90 Topps Rookies #11   3.00
❑ '90 Toys 'R' Us Rookies #13   2.00
❑ '90 Upper Deck #24 Team
    Checklist   1.00
❑ '90 Upper Deck #156   4.00
❑ '90 Wonder Bread Stars #18   5.00
❑ '91 Alrak Griffey Gazette set (4)   6.00
❑ '91 Bowman #246   1.50
❑ '91 Classic Game #120   2.00
❑ '91 Classic I #T3   1.25
❑ '91 Classic II #T1   1.25
❑ '91 Classic III #T30   1.00
❑ '91 Donruss #49 Ken Griffey Jr. AS   .75
❑ '91 Donruss #392 MVP   .75
❑ '91 Donruss #77   1.50
❑ '91 Donruss Previews #4   150.00
❑ '91 Fleer #450B   1.50
❑ '91 Fleer #450A   1.50
❑ '91 Fleer #710 w/ B. Bonds   .50
❑ '91 Fleer All-Stars #7   10.00
❑ '91 Jimmy Dean #2   3.00
❑ '91 Leaf #372   3.00
❑ '91 Mariners Country Hearth #15   6.00
❑ '91 Mariners Country Hearth #28

❑ w/ Ken Griffey Sr.   3.00
❑ '91 MooTown Snackers #4   3.00
❑ '91 Mother's Griffey Father/Son
    set (4)   6.00
❑ '91 O-Pee-Chee #392 AS   .75
❑ '91 O-Pee-Chee #790   1.50
❑ '91 OPC Premier #56   1.50
❑ '91 Pepsi Ken Griffey Jr./Sr. set (8) 9.00
❑ '91 Post #11   2.50
❑ '91 Score #2   1.50
❑ '91 Score #396 AS   .75
❑ '91 Score #697 Rifleman   .75
❑ '91 Score #841 w/ Ken Griffey Sr.   .75
❑ '91 Score #858 The Franchise   .75
❑ '91 Score #892 Dream Team   1.50
❑ '91 Score 100 Superstars #5   1.50
❑ '91 Score Cooperstown #B3   5.00
❑ '91 Stadium Club #270   15.00
❑ '91 Stadium Club Charter Member
    #10 w/ Ken Griffey Sr.   4.00
❑ '91 Studio #112   3.00
❑ '91 Sunflower Seeds #11   3.00
❑ '91 Topps #392 AS   .75
❑ '91 Topps #790   1.50
❑ '91 Topps Cracker Jack I #36   2.00
❑ '91 Topps Desert Shield #392 AS   60.00
❑ '91 Topps Desert Shield #790   120.00
❑ '91 Topps Tiffany #392 AS   4.00
❑ '91 Topps Tiffany #790   8.00
❑ '91 Ultra #336   3.00
❑ '91 Ultra Gold #4   6.00
❑ '91 Upper Deck #555   2.00
❑ '91 Upper Deck #572
    w/ Ken Griffey Sr.   .50
❑ '91 Upper Deck Final Edition
    #79F w/ R. Sandberg CL   .40
❑ '91 Upper Deck Final Edition #87F   .75
❑ '92 Alrak Griffey Golden Moments
    set (10)   18.00
❑ '92 Alrak Griffey McDonald's
    set (3)   10.00
❑ '92 Bowman #100   12.00
❑ '92 Classic Game #186   1.00
❑ '92 Classic I #T40   1.00
❑ '92 Classic II #T44   1.00
❑ '92 Classic/Best #AU1 autograph
    card; 3,100 signed   200.00
❑ '92 Classic/Best #200   1.00
❑ '92 Classic/Best Blue Bonus #BC12 3.00
❑ '92 Classic/Best Red Bonus #BC12   3.00
❑ '92 Colla All-Star Game #11   3.00
❑ '92 Donruss #24 AS   .75
❑ '92 Donruss #165   1.50
❑ '92 Donruss Cracker Jack I #12   2.00
❑ '92 Donruss Elite #13   150.00
❑ '92 Donruss Previews #7   100.00
❑ '92 Fleer #709 Pro-Visions   .75
❑ '92 Fleer #279   1.50
❑ '92 Fleer All-Stars #23   10.00
❑ '92 Fleer Citgo The Performer #4   1.50
❑ '92 Fleer Team Leaders #15   20.00
❑ '92 Fleer Update Headliners #H1   20.00
❑ '92 French's #15 w/ David Justice   1.50
❑ '92 Jimmy Dean #11   2.50
❑ '92 Leaf #392   2.50
❑ '92 Leaf Black Gold #392   12.00
❑ '92 Leaf Gold Previews #24   30.00

❑ '92 Leaf Previews #24	18.00
❑ '92 Mariners Mother's #2	4.00
❑ '92 MooTown Snackers #7	3.00
❑ '92 Mr. Turkey Superstars #12	3.00
❑ '92 O-Pee-Chee #50	1.00
❑ '92 OPC Premier #167	1.50
❑ '92 Pinnacle #283 w/ R. Henderson	.75
❑ '92 Pinnacle #549	3.00
❑ '92 Pinnacle Slugfest #7	10.00
❑ '92 Pinnacle Team 2000 #47	5.00
❑ '92 Pinnacle Team Pinnacle #9 w/ B. Butler	25.00
❑ '92 Post #20	2.50
❑ '92 Score #1	1.50
❑ '92 Score #436 AS	.75
❑ '92 Score 100 Superstars #1	1.50
❑ '92 Score Impact Players #28	4.00
❑ '92 Score Proctor and Gamble #7	2.50
❑ '92 Score Samples #1	8.00
❑ '92 Stadium Club #603 Members Choice	1.50
❑ '92 Stadium Club #400	3.00
❑ '92 Stadium Club Dome #70 AS	2.50
❑ '92 Stadium Club Master Photos #7	8.00
❑ '92 Stadium Club Members Only II #6	2.50
❑ '92 Studio #232	2.50
❑ '92 Sunflower Seeds #14	2.50
❑ '92 Topps #50	1.50
❑ '92 Topps Gold #50	20.00
❑ '92 Topps Gold Winners #50	8.00
❑ '92 Topps Kids #122	1.50
❑ '92 Topps McDonald's #8	6.00
❑ '92 Topps Micro #50	.75
❑ '92 Topps Micro Gold Insert #50	1.50
❑ '92 Triple Play #152	1.50
❑ '92 Triple Play Gallery #GS8	7.00
❑ '92 Triple Play Previews #1	75.00
❑ '92 Ultra #123	3.00
❑ '92 Ultra All-Stars #6	10.00
❑ '92 Ultra Award Winners #22	15.00
❑ '92 Upper Deck #85 w/ Craig	

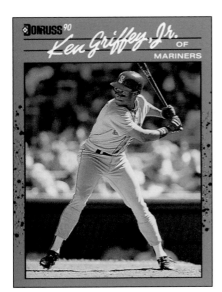

'90 Donruss Best AL #1

and Ken Griffey Sr.	.75
❑ '92 Upper Deck #424	1.50
❑ '92 Upper Deck #650 Diamond Skills	.75
❑ '92 Upper Deck All-Star FanFest #24	2.50
❑ '92 Upper Deck All-Star FanFest Gold #24	20.00
❑ '92 Upper Deck Team MVP Holograms #22	3.00
❑ '92 Upper Deck Williams Best #T15	8.00
❑ '93 Alrak Griffey 24 Taco Time set (6)	10.00
❑ '93 Alrak Griffey Triple Play #1	3.00
❑ '93 Bowman #375	3.00
❑ '93 Bowman #703 w/ Ken Griffey Sr.	1.00
❑ '93 Classic Game #38	1.00
❑ '93 Colla All-Star Game #3	3.00
❑ '93 Colla Diamond Marks #44	2.00
❑ '93 Colla Diamond Marks Art #3	30.00
❑ '93 Colla Diamond Marks Prototypes #5	30.00
❑ '93 Diamond Marks #44	2.00
❑ '93 Diamond Marks Art #3	30.00
❑ '93 Diamond Marks Prototypes #5	30.00
❑ '93 Donruss #553	2.00
❑ '93 Donruss Diamond Kings #DK1	12.00
❑ '93 Donruss Elite Dominators #7	150.00
❑ '93 Donruss Long Ball Leaders #LL9	25.00
❑ '93 Donruss Masters of the Game #8	10.00
❑ '93 Donruss MVPs #20	8.00
❑ '93 Donruss Previews #20	25.00
❑ '93 Duracell Power Players II #15	1.00
❑ '93 Finest #110	30.00
❑ '93 Finest All-Star Jumbos #110	60.00
❑ '93 Finest Refractors #110	1250.00
❑ '93 Flair #270	8.00
❑ '93 Fleer #307	2.00
❑ '93 Fleer All-Stars #AL7	12.00
❑ '93 Fleer Atlantic #11	1.50
❑ '93 Fleer Fruit of the Loom #25	10.00
❑ '93 Fleer Team Leaders #AL10	20.00
❑ '93 Fun Pack #224 CL	1.00
❑ '93 Fun Pack #111 Glow Stars	1.00
❑ '93 Fun Pack #16 Hot Shots	4.00
❑ '93 Fun Pack #24 Kid Stars	1.00
❑ '93 Fun Pack #30 Upper Deck Heroes	1.00
❑ '93 Fun Pack #114	2.00
❑ '93 Fun Pack All-Stars #AS8 w/ M. Grissom	4.00
❑ '93 Hostess #25	1.50
❑ '93 Jimmy Dean #11	2.50
❑ '93 Kraft #8	4.00
❑ '93 Leaf #3'	3.00
❑ '93 Leaf Gold All-Stars #R7 w/ A. Van Slyke	6.00
❑ '93 Leaf Gold All-Stars #U8 w/ M. Grissom	5.00
❑ '93 Mariners Mother's #4	3.00
❑ '93 Metz Baking #9	2.00

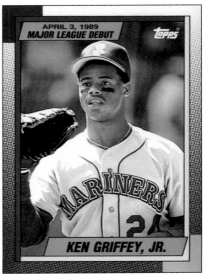

'90 Topps Debut '89 #46

❑ '93 O-Pee-Chee #91	3.00
❑ '93 OPC Premier Star Performers #9	2.00
❑ '93 OPC Premier Star Performers Foil #9	50.00
❑ '93 Pacific Jugadores Calientes #7	20.00
❑ '93 Pacific Spanish #286	2.00
❑ '93 Pinnacle #110	3.00
❑ '93 Pinnacle Cooperstown #22	2.00
❑ '93 Pinnacle Cooperstown Dufex #22	250.00
❑ '93 Pinnacle Home Run Club #13	4.00
❑ '93 Pinnacle Slugfest #28	15.00
❑ '93 Post #7	2.50
❑ '93 Score #1	2.00
❑ '93 Score #504 AS	1.00
❑ '93 Score #536 Dream Team	1.00
❑ '93 Score Franchise #12	35.00
❑ '93 Score Gold Dream Team #5	2.00
❑ '93 Select #2	3.00
❑ '93 Select Chase Stars #'	50.00
❑ '93 Select Stat Leaders #15	2.00
❑ '93 SP #4	8.00
❑ '93 SP Platinum Power #PP9	60.00
❑ '93 Stadium Club #591 Members Choice	1.50
❑ '93 Stadium Club #707	3.00
❑ '93 Stadium Club First Day Issue #591 Members Choice	60.00
❑ '93 Stadium Club First Day Issue #707	120.00
❑ '93 Stadium Club Inserts #B4 w/ D. Strawberry	4.00
❑ '93 Stadium Club Mariners #1	3.00
❑ '93 Stadium Club Master Photos #26	5.00
❑ '93 Stadium Club Members Only #11	3.50
❑ '93 Stadium Club Members Only parallel #591 Members Choice	5.00
❑ '93 Stadium Club Members Only parallel #707	10.00
❑ '93 Stadium Club Murphy #56 AS	3.00

❏ '93 Stadium Club Murphy Master Photos #3 AS	3.00
❏ '93 Studio #96	2.50
❏ '93 Studio Superstars on Canvas #1	15.00
❏ '93 Topps #405 w/ A.Van Slyke AS	.50
❏ '93 Topps #179	2.00
❏ '93 Topps Black Gold #33	3.00
❏ '93 Topps Full Shots #2	10.00
❏ '93 Topps Gold #405 w/ A.Van Slyke AS	1.50
❏ '93 Topps Gold #179	6.00
❏ '93 Topps Marlins Inaugural #179	6.00
❏ '93 Topps Marlins Inaugural #405 w/ A.Van Slyke AS	1.50
❏ '93 Topps Micro Prism Inserts #179	1.25
❏ '93 Topps Pre-Production #179	2.50
❏ '93 Topps Rockies Inaugural #179	6.00
❏ '93 Topps Rockies Inaugural #405 w/ A.Van Slyke AS	1.50
❏ '93 Toys 'R'Us #1	3.00
❏ '93 Toys 'R' Us Master Photos #5	2.00
❏ '93 Triple Play #1	2.00
❏ '93 Triple Play Action #24	2.00
❏ '93 Triple Play Nicknames #5	12.00
❏ '93 Ultra #619	3.00
❏ '93 Ultra All-Stars #17	15.00
❏ '93 Ultra Award Winners #16	15.00
❏ '93 Ultra Performers #3	8.00
❏ '93 Upper Deck #525 CL	0.15
❏ '93 Upper Deck #55 w/ Buhner and Mitchell	.50
❏ '93 Upper Deck #355	2.00
❏ '93 Upper Deck Clutch Performers #R11	5.00
❏ '93 Upper Deck Diamond Gallery #13	3.00
❏ '93 Upper Deck Fifth Anniversary #A1	8.00
❏ '93 Upper Deck Fifth Anniversary Jumbo #A1	16.00
❏ '93 Upper Deck Future Heroes #59	5.00

'92 Donruss Elite #13

❏ '93 Upper Deck Gold Hologram #55 w/ Buhner and Mitchell	.75
❏ '93 Upper Deck Gold Hologram #355	3.00
❏ '93 Upper Deck Gold Hologram #525 CL	.25
❏ '93 Upper Deck Home Run Heroes #HR9	5.00
❏ '93 Upper Deck Iooss Collection #WI13	6.00
❏ '93 Upper Deck Iooss Collection Jumbo #WI13	12.00
❏ '93 Upper Deck On Deck #D13	5.00
❏ '93 Upper Deck Season Highlights #HI9	50.00
❏ '93 Upper Deck Triple Crown #TC4	10.00
❏ '94 Bowman #5	3.00
❏ '94 Bowman's Best #X96 w/ J. Damon	6.00
❏ '94 Bowman's Best #R40	10.00
❏ '94 Bowman's Best Refractors #X96 w/ J. Damon	36.00
❏ '94 Bowman's Best Refractors #R40	100.00
❏ '94 Church's Show Stoppers #3	10.00
❏ '94 Collector's Choice #117	2.00
❏ '94 Collector's Choice #317 CL	.50
❏ '94 Collector's Choice #324 CL	.50
❏ '94 Collector's Choice #340 Team Checklist	1.00
❏ '94 Collector's Choice #634 Up Close	1.00
❏ '94 Collector's Choice Gold Signature #117	125.00
❏ '94 Collector's Choice Gold Signature #317 CL	30.00
❏ '94 Collector's Choice Gold Signature #324 CL	30.00
❏ '94 Collector's Choice Gold Signature #340 Team Checklist	60.00
❏ '94 Collector's Choice Gold Signature #634 Up Close	60.00
❏ '94 Collector's Choice Home Run All-S #HA2	3.00
❏ '94 Collector's Choice Jumbo Promo	3.00
❏ '94 Collector's Choice Promo #50	3.00
❏ '94 Collector's Choice Silver Signature #117	12.00
❏ '94 Collector's Choice Silver Signature #317 CL	3.00
❏ '94 Collector's Choice Silver Signature #324 CL	3.00
❏ '94 Collector's Choice Silver Signature #340 Team Checklist	6.00
❏ '94 Collector's Choice Silver Signature #634 Up Close	6.00
❏ '94 Collector's Choice Team vs. Team #2 w/ B. Bonds	1.00
❏ '94 Collector's Choice Team vs. Team #7 w/ J. Gonzalez	1.00
❏ '94 Dairy Queen Ken Griffey Jr. set (10)	7.50
❏ '94 Denny's Holograms #12	8.00
❏ '94 Donruss #4	3.00
❏ '94 Donruss Diamond Kings #14	10.00

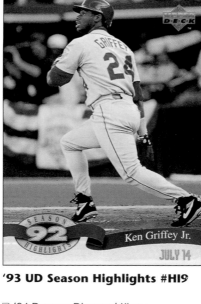

'93 UD Season Highlights #HI9

❏ '94 Donruss Diamond Kings Jumbo #14	20.00
❏ '94 Donruss Dominators #A9	10.00
❏ '94 Donruss Dominators #B6	10.00
❏ '94 Donruss Dominators Jumbo #A9	20.00
❏ '94 Donruss Dominators Jumbo #B6	20.00
❏ '94 Donruss Elite #45	60.00
❏ '94 Donruss Long Ball Leaders #5	15.00
❏ '94 Donruss MVPs #26	15.00
❏ '94 Donruss Promos #7	10.00
❏ '94 Donruss Special Edition #4	6.00
❏ '94 Donruss Spirit of the Game #3	20.00
❏ '94 Extra Bases #166	3.00
❏ '94 Extra Bases Game Breakers #14	5.00
❏ '94 Finest #232	12.00
❏ '94 Finest Jumbos #232	40.00
❏ '94 Finest Refractors #232	125.00
❏ '94 Flair #103	5.00
❏ '94 Flair Hot Gloves #3	125.00
❏ '94 Flair Outfield Power #6	12.00
❏ '94 Fleer #286	3.00
❏ '94 Fleer All-Stars #10	4.00
❏ '94 Fleer Golden Moments #4	12.00
❏ '94 Fleer Golden Moments Jumbo #4	12.00
❏ '94 Fleer Lumber Company #5	5.00
❏ '94 Fleer Sunoco #13	1.25
❏ '94 Fleer Team Leaders #12	5.00
❏ '94 Fun Pack #235 CL	1.50
❏ '94 Fun Pack #224 Foldouts	1.50
❏ '94 Fun Pack #229 Fun Cards	1.50
❏ '94 Fun Pack #'3 Pro-Files	1.50
❏ '94 Fun Pack #182 Standouts	1.50
❏ '94 Fun Pack #200 w/ Mattingly Headline Stars	2.00
❏ '94 Fun Pack #216 What's the Call?	1.50
❏ '94 Fun Pack #24	3.00
❏ '94 Fun Pack Promo #24	3.00
❏ '94 Kraft #5	4.00
❏ '94 Leaf #368	3.00
❏ '94 Leaf Gamers #1	60.00

❏ '94 Leaf Gold Stars #4	60.00
❏ '94 Leaf Limited #66	10.00
❏ '94 Leaf Limited Gold All-Stars #11	50.00
❏ '94 Leaf MVP Contenders #A8	35.00
❏ '94 Leaf MVP Contenders Gold#A8	45.00
❏ '94 Leaf Power Brokers #5	8.00
❏ '94 Leaf Promos #3	6.00
❏ '94 Leaf Slideshow #9	20.00
❏ '94 Leaf Statistical Standouts #6	5.00
❏ '94 Mariners Mother's #4	7.00
❏ '94 O-Pee-Chee #22	2.00
❏ '94 O-Pee-Chee All-Star Redemptions #8	2.00
❏ '94 O-Pee-Chee All-Star Redemptions Jumbo #8	12.00
❏ '94 O-Pee-Chee All-Star Redemptions Jumbo Foil #8	12.00
❏ '94 Pacific #570	2.00
❏ '94 Pacific Gold Prisms #2	25.00
❏ '94 Pacific Promos #P4	12.00
❏ '94 Pacific Silver Prisms #8	20.00
❏ '94 Pacific Silver Prisms circular background #8	10.00
❏ '94 Pinnacle #100	3.00
❏ '94 Pinnacle Artist's Proofs #100	125.00
❏ '94 Pinnacle Museum Collection #100	50.00
❏ '94 Pinnacle Power Surge #23	2.00
❏ '94 Pinnacle Run Creators #RC3	20.00
❏ '94 Pinnacle Team Pinnacle #6 w/ L. Dykstra	40.00
❏ '94 Pinnacle The Naturals #3	4.00
❏ '94 Pinnacle Tribute #TR17	20.00
❏ '94 Post #15	2.00
❏ '94 Post Canadian #10	2.50
❏ '94 Score #3	2.00
❏ '94 Score #628 Highlights	1.00
❏ '94 Score Cycle #TC17	60.00
❏ '94 Score Gold Rush #3	12.00
❏ '94 Score Gold Rush #628 Highlights	6.00
❏ '94 Score Gold Stars #32	40.00
❏ '94 Score Samples #3GR	12.00
❏ '94 Score Samples #3	4.00
❏ '94 Select #1	3.00
❏ '94 Select Crown Contenders #CC10	25.00
❏ '94 Signature Rookies Flip Cards #2 w/ Craig	5.00
❏ '94 Signature Rookies Flip Cards #3 w/ Ken Griffey Sr.	7.00
❏ '94 Signature Rookies Flip Cards Signatures #AU2 w/ Craig signed 1,000	20.00
❏ '94 Signature Rookies Flip Cards Signatures #AU5 w/ Craig; Ken signed 500	300.00
❏ '94 Signature Rookies Flip Cards Signatures #AU4 w/ Ken Griffey Sr. signed 1,000	25.00
❏ '94 Signature Rookies Flip Cards Signatures #AU6 w/ Ken Griffey Sr.; Ken Jr. signed 500	300.00
❏ '94 SP #105	5.00
❏ '94 SP Diecut #105	15.00
❏ '94 SP Holoview Blue #12	30.00
❏ '94 SP Holoview Red #12	350.00

❏ '94 SP Previews #WR3	30.00
❏ '94 SP Promo #24	3.00
❏ '94 Sportflics #143	3.00
❏ '94 Sportflics #181 Starflics	1.50
❏ '94 Sportflics FanFest All-Stars #AS7 w/ L. Dykstra	10.00
❏ '94 Sportflics R/T Going Going Gone #GG4	25.00
❏ '94 Stadium Club #85	3.00
❏ '94 Stadium Club #262 HR Club	1.50
❏ '94 Stadium Club #529 Division Leaders	1.50
❏ '94 Stadium Club Dugout Dirt #7	3.00
❏ '94 Stadium Club Finest #5	10.00
❏ '94 Stadium Club First Day Issue #85	100.00
❏ '94 Stadium Club First Day Issue #262 HR Club	50.00
❏ '94 Stadium Club First Day Issue #529 Division Leaders	50.00
❏ '94 Stadium Club Golden Rainbow #85	12.00
❏ '94 Stadium Club Golden Rainbow #262 HR Club	6.00
❏ '94 Stadium Club Golden Rainbow #529 Division Leaders	6.00
❏ '94 Stadium Club Members Only #17	3.50
❏ '94 Stadium Club Members Only #85	10.00
❏ '94 Stadium Club Members Only #262 HR Club	5.00
❏ '94 Stadium Club Members Only #529 Division Leaders	5.00
❏ '94 Studio #101	3.00
❏ '94 Studio Editor's Choice #3	15.00
❏ '94 Studio Series Stars #4	45.00
❏ '94 Tombstone Pizza #21	3.00
❏ '94 Topps #388 w/ L. Dykstra AS	.50
❏ '94 Topps #400	2.00
❏ '94 Topps #606 Stat Twins	1.00
❏ '94 Topps Black Gold #8	4.00
❏ '94 Topps Gold #388 w/ L. Dykstra AS	1.50
❏ '94 Topps Gold #400	6.00
❏ '94 Topps Gold #606 Stat Twins	3.00
❏ '94 Topps Spanish #606 Stat Twins	3.00
❏ '94 Topps Spanish #388 w/ L. Dykstra AS	1.50
❏ '94 Topps Spanish #400	6.00
❏ '94 Topps Superstar Samplers cello pack #19	20.00
❏ '94 Topps Traded Finest #5	10.00
❏ '94 Triple Play #127	2.00
❏ '94 Triple Play Bomb Squad #8	12.00
❏ '94 Triple Play Medalists #11 w/ Puckett and Belle	10.00
❏ '94 Triple Play Promos #4	6.00
❏ '94 Ultra #120	3.00
❏ '94 Ultra All-Stars #8	5.00
❏ '94 Ultra Award Winners #6	5.00
❏ '94 Ultra Home Run Kings #2	25.00
❏ '94 Ultra On-Base Leaders #6	75.00
❏ '94 Upper Deck #KG Autograph; 1,000 signed	250.00
❏ '94 Upper Deck #GM w/ Mantle Autograph;	

1,000 signed by both	1000.00
❏ '94 Upper Deck #53 Future is Now	1.50
❏ '94 Upper Deck #224	3.00
❏ '94 Upper Deck #292 Home Field Advantage	1.50
❏ '94 Upper Deck All-Star Jumbos #1	4.00
❏ '94 Upper Deck All-Star Jumbos #48 125th Ann.	2.00
❏ '94 Upper Deck All-Star Jumbos Gold #1	32.00
❏ '94 Upper Deck All-Star Jumbos Gold #48 125th Ann.	16.00
❏ '94 Upper Deck All-Star Jumbos Promo #48	3.00
❏ '94 Upper Deck Diamond Collection #W4	50.00
❏ '94 Upper Deck Electric Diamond #53 Future is Now	5.00
❏ '94 Upper Deck Electric Diamond #224	10.00
❏ '94 Upper Deck Electric Diamond #292 Home Field Advantage	5.00
❏ '94 Upper Deck Ken Griffey Jumbos set (4)	20.00
❏ '94 Upper Deck Mantle's Long Shots #MM10	10.00
❏ '94 Upper Deck Mantle's Long Shots Electric Diamond #MM10	12.50
❏ '94 Upper Deck Next Generation #6	20.00
❏ '94 Upper Deck Next Generation Electric Diamond #6	25.00
❏ '94 Upper Deck Promo #224	3.00
❏ '94 Upper Deck Top Ten Promo #6	3.00
❏ '95 Bazooka #31	2.00
❏ '95 Bazooka Red Hot #RH7	4.00
❏ '95 Bowman #321	3.00
❏ '95 Bowman's Best #X12 w/ Todd Greene	4.00
❏ '95 Bowman's Best #R49	8.00
❏ '95 Bowman's Best Refractors/ Diffraction Foil #X12 w/ Todd Greene	20.00

'94 Leaf Gamers #1

❑ '95 Bowman's Best Refractors/
    Diffraction Foil #R49   80.00
❑ '95 Collector's Choice #62 Best
    of the '90s   1.00
❑ '95 Collector's Choice #70   2.00
❑ '95 Collector's Choice #88
    What's the Call?   1.00
❑ '95 Collector's Choice Crash
    the Game #CG8B Aug 24   2.00
❑ '95 Collector's Choice Crash
    the Game #CG8A July 2   2.00
❑ '95 Collector's Choice Crash
    the Game #CG8C Sept 15   2.00
❑ '95 Collector's Choice Crash
    the Game Gold #CG8B Aug 24   10.00
❑ '95 Collector's Choice Crash
    the Game Gold #CG8A July 2   10.00
❑ '95 Collector's Choice Crash
    the Game Gold #CG8C Sept 15   10.00
❑ '95 Collector's Choice Gold
    Signature #62 Best of the '90s   25.00
❑ '95 Collector's Choice Gold
    Signature #70   50.00
❑ '95 Collector's Choice Gold
    Signature #88 What's the Call?   25.00
❑ '95 Collector's Choice Promo #172   3.00
❑ '95 Collector's Choice SE #261 CL   1.00
❑ '95 Collector's Choice SE #26
    Record Pace   1.50
❑ '95 Collector's Choice SE #125   3.00
❑ '95 Collector's Choice SE Gold
    Signature #261 CL   40.00
❑ '95 Collector's Choice SE Gold
    Signature #26 Record Pace   60.00
❑ '95 Collector's Choice SE Gold
    Signature #125   125.00
❑ '95 Collector's Choice SE Promo
    #125   3.00
❑ '95 Collector's Choice SE Silver
    Signature #261 CL   3.00
❑ '95 Collector's Choice SE Silver
    Signature #26 Record Pace   5.00
❑ '95 Collector's Choice SE Silver

'95 Collector's Choice #70

    Signature #125   10.00
❑ '95 Collector's Choice Silver
    Signature #62 Best of the '90s   4.00
❑ '95 Collector's Choice Silver
    Signature #88 What's the Call?   4.00
❑ '95 Collector's Choice Silver
    Signature #70   8.00
❑ '95 D3 #43   4.00
❑ '95 Denny's Holograms #11   5.00
❑ '95 Donruss #340   3.00
❑ '95 Donruss All-Stars #AL8   40.00
❑ '95 Donruss Bomb Squad #1
    w/ M. Williams   9.00
❑ '95 Donruss Diamond Kings
    #DK27   12.00
❑ '95 Donruss Dominators #8
    w/ Lofton and Grissom   10.00
❑ '95 Donruss Elite #54   75.00
❑ '95 Donruss Long Ball Leaders #3   8.00
❑ '95 Donruss Press Proofs #340   125.00
❑ '95 Embossed #51   3.00
❑ '95 Embossed Golden Idols #51   12.00
❑ '95 Emotion #77   5.00
❑ '95 Emotion Masters #3   20.00
❑ '95 Emotion N-Tense #6   65.00
❑ '95 Finest #118   10.00
❑ '95 Finest Power Kings #PK10   60.00
❑ '95 Finest Refractors #118   375.00
❑ '95 Flair #81   5.00
❑ '95 Flair Hot Gloves #3   90.00
❑ '95 Flair Hot Numbers #4   15.00
❑ '95 Flair Outfield Power #7   8.00
❑ '95 Fleer #269   3.00
❑ '95 Fleer All-Fleer #7   3.00
❑ '95 Fleer All-Stars #7 w/ T. Gwynn   4.00
❑ '95 Fleer League Leaders #2   5.00
❑ '95 Fleer Lumber Company #6   15.00
❑ '95 Fleer Team Leaders #12
    w/ R. Johnson   45.00
❑ '95 Fleer Update Diamond Tribute
    #6   3.00
❑ '95 Fleer Update Headliners #11   3.00
❑ '95 Fleer Update Smooth Leather
    #3   12.00
❑ '95 Kraft #5   4.00
❑ '95 Leaf #211   3.00
❑ '95 Leaf 300 Club #10   35.00
❑ '95 Leaf Gold Stars #4   60.00
❑ '95 Leaf Great Gloves #6   3.00
❑ '95 Leaf Heading for the Hall #2   120.00
❑ '95 Leaf Limited #118   10.00
❑ '95 Leaf Limited Bat Patrol #5   12.00
❑ '95 Leaf Limited Gold #6   12.00
❑ '95 Leaf Limited Lumberjacks #4   120.00
❑ '95 Leaf Opening Day #4   3.00
❑ '95 Leaf Slideshow #8   15.00
❑ '95 Leaf Statistical Standouts #2   140.00
❑ '95 Mariners Mother's #4   7.00
❑ '95 National Packtime #6   3.00
❑ '95 Pacific #398   2.00
❑ '95 Pacific Gold Crown Diecuts #16   50.00
❑ '95 Pacific Gold Prisms #21   25.00
❑ '95 Pacific Prisms #126   20.00
❑ '95 Pinnacle #128   3.00
❑ '95 Pinnacle #304 Swingmen   1.50
❑ '95 Pinnacle #447 CL   1.50
❑ '95 Pinnacle #450 w/ Bagwell,

'95 Leaf Statistical Standout #2

    Piazza, Thomas CL   2.00
❑ '95 Pinnacle Artist's Proofs #128   125.00
❑ '95 Pinnacle Artist's Proofs #304
    Swingmen   60.00
❑ '95 Pinnacle Artist's Proofs #447
    CL   60.00
❑ '95 Pinnacle Artist's Proofs #450
    w/ Bagwell, Piazza, Thomas CL   110.00
❑ '95 Pinnacle FanFest #11   5.00
❑ '95 Pinnacle Gate Attractions
    #GA1   30.00
❑ '95 Pinnacle Museum Collection
    #128   50.00
❑ '95 Pinnacle Museum Collection
    #304 Swingmen   25.00
❑ '95 Pinnacle Museum Collection
    #447 CL   25.00
❑ '95 Pinnacle Museum Collection
    #450 w/ Bagwell, Piazza, Thomas
    CL   45.00
❑ '95 Pinnacle Pin Redemption #14   25.00
❑ '95 Pinnacle Red Hot #2   20.00
❑ '95 Pinnacle Team Pinnacle #TP7
    Bonds side dufex   60.00
❑ '95 Pinnacle Team Pinnacle #TP7
    Griffey side dufex   75.00
❑ '95 Pinnacle White Hot #2   80.00
❑ '95 Score #437   2.00
❑ '95 Score #551 Hit Men   1.00
❑ '95 Score Double Gold Champs
    #GC2   25.00
❑ '95 Score Dream Team #DG7   40.00
❑ '95 Score Gold Rush #437   12.00
❑ '95 Score Gold Rush #551 Hit Men   6.00
❑ '95 Score Hall of Gold #HG1   12.00
❑ '95 Score Platinum #437   35.00
❑ '95 Score Rules #SR1   40.00
❑ '95 Score Rules Jumbo #SR1   20.00
❑ '95 Select #89   2.00
❑ '95 Select #243 CL   1.00
❑ '95 Select #250 w/ Bagwell,
    Piazza, Thomas CL   1.50
❑ '95 Select Artist's Proofs #89   325.00

❏ '95 Select Artist's Proofs #243 CL 150.00
❏ '95 Select Artist's Proofs #250
   w/ Bagwell, Piazza, Thomas CL 275.00
❏ '95 Select Big Sticks #BS2   50.00
❏ '95 Select Certified #70   5.00
❏ '95 Select Certified Checklists #1   1.00
❏ '95 Select Certified Gold Team #1   75.00
❏ '95 Select Certified Mirror Gold
   #70   60.00
❏ '95 SP #'0   4.00
❏ '95 SP Championship #183 Major
   League Profiles   2.00
❏ '95 SP Championship #185   4.00
❏ '95 SP Championship Diecuts
   #183 Major League Profiles   6.00
❏ '95 SP Championship Diecuts
   #185   12.00
❏ '95 SP Championship Fall Classic
   #1   40.00
❏ '95 SP Championship Fall Classic
   Diecuts #1   120.00
❏ '95 SP Platinum Power #PP12   8.00
❏ '95 SP Silver #'0   12.00
❏ '95 SP Special FX #18   250.00
❏ '95 Sportflix #1   3.00
❏ '95 Sportflix #168 CL   1.50
❏ '95 Sportflix Artist's Proofs #1   125.00
❏ '95 Sportflix Artist's Proofs #168
   CL   60.00
❏ '95 Sportflix Detonators #DE3   10.00
❏ '95 Sportflix Double Take #9
   w/ B. Bonds   32.00
❏ '95 Sportflix Hammer Team
   #HT1   5.00
❏ '95 Sportflix ProMotion #PM1   40.00
❏ '95 Stadium Club #241   3.00
❏ '95 Stadium Club #521 Extreme
   Corps   1.50
❏ '95 Stadium Club Clear Cut #18   25.00
❏ '95 Stadium Club Crunch Time #9   10.00
❏ '95 Stadium Club First Day Issue
   #241   40.00
❏ '95 Stadium Club First Day Issue
   #521 Extreme Corps   20.00
❏ '95 Stadium Club Members Only
   #19   3.00
❏ '95 Stadium Club Power Zone
   #PZ7   30.00
❏ '95 Stadium Club Ring Leaders
   #14   30.00
❏ '95 Stadium Club Super Skills
   #11   25.00
❏ '95 Stadium Club Virtual
   Extremists #VRE2   40.00
❏ '95 Stadium Club Virtual Reality
   #120   6.00
❏ '95 Studio #5   4.00
❏ '95 Studio Gold Series #5   6.00
❏ '95 Studio Platinum Series #5   24.00
❏ '95 Summit #1   3.00
❏ '95 Summit #174 Bat Speed   1.50
❏ '95 Summit #195 CL   1.50
❏ '95 Summit Big Bang #BB1   90.00
❏ '95 Summit Nth Degree #1   50.00
❏ '95 Summit Nth Degree #174
   Bat Speed   25.00
❏ '95 Summit Nth Degree #195 CL   25.00

❏ '95 Tombstone Pizza #9   2.50
❏ '95 Topps #388 w/ B. Bonds AS   .60
❏ '95 Topps #397   3.00
❏ '95 Topps Cyberstats #'9   8.00
❏ '95 Topps Finest #3   20.00
❏ '95 Topps League Leaders #LL31   6.00
❏ '95 Topps Traded #2 At the Break   1.50
❏ '95 Topps Traded #160
   w/ T. Gwynn AS   .50
❏ '95 Topps Traded Power Boosters
   #2   30.00
❏ '95 UC3 #73   3.00
❏ '95 UC3 #124 In Depth   1.50
❏ '95 UC3 Artist's Proofs #73   125.00
❏ '95 UC3 Artist's Proofs #124
   In Depth   60.00
❏ '95 UC3 Cyclone Squad #CS2   5.00
❏ '95 UC3 In Motion #IM2   12.00
❏ '95 Ultra #101   3.00
❏ '95 Ultra All-Stars #7   5.00
❏ '95 Ultra All-Stars Gold Medallion
   #7   15.00
❏ '95 Ultra Award Winners #6   5.00
❏ '95 Ultra Award Winners Gold
   Medallion #6   15.00
❏ '95 Ultra Gold Medallion #101   12.00
❏ '95 Ultra Hitting Machines #6   5.00
❏ '95 Ultra Hitting Machines Gold
   Medallion #6   15.00
❏ '95 Ultra Home Run Kings #1   12.00
❏ '95 Ultra Home Run Kings Gold
   Medallion #1   36.00
❏ '95 Ultra Power Plus #2   20.00
❏ '95 Ultra Power Plus Gold
   Medallion #2   60.00
❏ '95 Upper Deck #100   3.00
❏ '95 Upper Deck #110 Analysis   1.50
❏ '95 Upper Deck Electric Diamond
   #100   12.00
❏ '95 Upper Deck Electric Diamond
   #110 Analysis   6.00
❏ '95 Upper Deck Electric Diamond
   Gold #100   100.00
❏ '95 Upper Deck Electric Diamond
   Gold #110 Analysis   50.00
❏ '95 Upper Deck Predictor Award
   Winners #H3 MVP   15.00
❏ '95 Upper Deck Predictor League
   Leaders #R52 Batting   15.00
❏ '95 Upper Deck Predictor League
   Leaders #R4 HR   15.00
❏ '95 Upper Deck Predictor League
   Leaders #R45 RBI   15.00
❏ '95 Upper Deck Special Edition
   #255   10.00
❏ '95 Upper Deck Special Edition
   Gold #255   125.00
❏ '95 Zenith #61   5.00
❏ '95 Zenith All-Star Salute #15   10.00
❏ '95 Zenith Z-Team #2   175.00
❏ '96 Collector's Choice #310   2.00
❏ '96 Collector's Choice Gold
   Signature #310   50.00
❏ '96 Collector's Choice Silver
   Signature #310   8.00
❏ '96 Collector's Choice
   You Make the Play #16   2.00

❏ '96 Collector's Choice You Make
   the Play Gold Signature #16   30.00
❏ '96 Donruss Hit List #2   50.00
❏ '96 Donruss Long Ball Leaders #6   75.00
❏ '96 Donruss Power Alley #10   75.00
❏ '96 Donruss Power Alley Diecuts
   #10   300.00
❏ '96 Donruss Samples #4   2.50
❏ '96 Donruss Showdown #3
   w/ G. Maddux   60.00
❏ '96 Score #273 CL   1.00
❏ '96 Score Big Bats #2   30.00
❏ '96 Score Diamond Aces #14   20.00
❏ '96 Score Dream Team #7   30.00
❏ '96 Score Numbers Game #3   10.00
❏ '96 Score Reflextions #2
   w/ A. Rodriguez   20.00
❏ '96 Topps #205   3.00
❏ '96 Topps Classic Confrontations
   #CC1   .75
❏ '96 Topps Finest #M16   30.00
❏ '96 Topps Finest #M25   30.00
❏ '96 Topps Finest Refractors #M16   90.00
❏ '96 Topps Finest Refractors #M25   90.00
❏ '96 Topps Profiles #AL5   5.00
❏ '96 Ultra #126   3.00
❏ '96 Ultra Checklists #4   3.00
❏ '96 Ultra Checklists Gold
   Medallion #4   9.00
❏ '96 Ultra Diamond Producers #3   15.00
❏ '96 Ultra Diamond Producers
   Gold Medallion #3   45.00
❏ '96 Ultra Gold Medallion #126   12.00
❏ '96 Ultra Home Run Kings #6   50.00
❏ '96 Ultra Home Run Kings Gold
   Medallion #6   150.00
❏ '96 Ultra Power Plus #3   10.00
❏ '96 Ultra Power Plus Gold
   Medallion #3   30.00
❏ '96 Ultra Prime Leather #6   12.00
❏ '96 Ultra Prime Leather Gold
   Medallion #6   36.00
❏ '96 Ultra Samples #2   4.00

'96 Donruss Hit List #2

Peace

inner

In a sport that's too often beating up on itself, boy-at-heart Ken Griffey Jr. offers the game and its fans something it's been missing . . . .

MEL BAILEY

Happy Days

Whether he's warming up with his team-mates, hanging out in the dugout or swapping stories with an opponent, Junior gets a kick out of just being at the ballpark. No matter the score, Junior seems to have more fun than anyone else in baseball.

MITCHELL HADDAD

The Cat in the Hat

Some purists suggest Junior shows disrespect for the game by turning his hat around for batting practice. But by sporting his signature style while winning the '94 home run contest at the All-Star Game, Griffey made it clear that he's still headed in the right direction.

KEN GRIFFEY JR.

MITCHELL B. REIBEL / SPORTS PHOTO MASTERS

STEPHEN DUNN / ALLSPORT USA

Down to Business

From his first day at the Mariners' training camp, Junior has had one goal: winning baseball games. Griffey's first few years in Seattle didn't quench his thirst for success, but now that he's tasted the playoffs, he plans on revisiting that oasis time and time again.

FOCUS ON SPORTS

AP / WIDE WORLD PHOTOS

Up, Up and Away

This Griffey pose has become an all-too-familiar scene for many American League pitchers. Just one mistake is all it takes for Junior to blast a pitch into the stratosphere before it finally drops into the outfield bleachers.

JEFF CARLICK / MLB PHOTOS

seasons
IN THE sun

Reviewing the key events of each of
Ken Griffey Jr.'s seven major league seasons

1989

- Made club as non-roster player by hitting .359 in spring training. Established new team spring training records with 33 hits, 21 RBI and a 15-game hitting streak.
- Doubled off Oakland's Dave Stewart in first major league at-bat on April 3.
- First major league home run came on first pitch he saw in Kingdome, off Chicago's Eric King on April 10.
- Tied Seattle record with eight consecutive hits from April 23 to April 26.
- Set team record by reaching base safely 11 straight times April 23-27.
- Won game with two-run homer off Milwaukee's Bill Wegman in first major league pinch-hit appearance.
- Fashioned an 11-game hitting streak from June 14 to June 25.
- Hit inside-the-park homer in New York off Clay Parker on May 21.
- Was on disabled list from July 25 to Aug. 20 with broken bone in little finger of right hand.
- Led AL outfielders with six double plays and finished fifth in assists with 12.
- At age 19, was the youngest player in the major leagues.

Year	Team	Avg.	G	AB	R	H	2B	3B	HR	RBI	BB	SO	SB
1989	Seattle	.264	127	455	61	120	23	0	16	61	44	83	16

KEN GRIFFEY JR.

TOM DIPACE

1990

- Robbed New York's Jesse Barfield of his 200th career home run with an over-the-wall catch in the fourth inning at Yankee Stadium on April 26.
- Named AL Player of the Month for April after hitting .388 with five homers and 17 RBI.
- Became first Mariner ever voted into the starting lineup of the All-Star Game after receiving 2,159,700 votes, second to Oakland's Jose Canseco.
- At age 20, was second-youngest player ever to start in the All-Star Game.
- Played professionally with his father for the first time on Aug. 31 against Kansas City.
- He and his father hit back-to-back homers in the first inning at California off Kirk McCaskill on Sept. 14.
- Finished fourth in the AL in total bases (287) and led Mariners in homers (22) and RBI (87).
- Earned his first Gold Glove Award, becoming the second-youngest player ever to win the award.

Year	Team	Avg.	G	AB	R	H	2B	3B	HR	RBI	BB	SO	SB
1990	Seattle	.300	155	597	91	179	28	7	22	80	63	81	16

1991

- Robbed Texas' Ruben Sierra of extra bases with a backhanded catch at full gallop an instant before he crashed feet-first into the Kingdome wall in right-center on May 25.
- Finished as the AL's leading vote-getter for the All-Star Game with 2,248,396 votes.
- Tied club record with five hits against Milwaukee on July 18.
- Hit first career grand slam July 23 at Yankee Stadium off Lee Guetterman.
- Batted .434 in July, and hit in 11 straight games from July 21 to Aug. 4.
- Collected his 100th RBI on Sept. 30 in Texas, becoming the youngest player to reach that milestone since Al Kaline in 1956.
- Hit .372 with 13 homers and 64 RBI after the All-Star break.
- Set new club records for batting average (.327), doubles (42), slugging percentage (.527), intentional walks (21) and grand-slam homers (three).
- Won second straight Gold Glove and first Silver Slugger awards.

Year	Team	Avg.	G	AB	R	H	2B	3B	HR	RBI	BB	SO	SB
1991	Seattle	.327	154	548	76	179	42	1	22	100	71	82	18

RON VESELY

1992

- Collected career-high five RBI at Milwaukee on April 19.
- Homered on consecutive pitches from Toronto's Jack Morris on May 7, the fourth two-homer game of his career.
- Sprained right wrist diving for a catch and went on disabled list from July 9 to July 24.
- After receiving third-highest vote total (2,071,407), was named MVP of All-Star Game after going 3-for-3 and hitting home run off Chicago's Greg Maddux.
- Equaled career high with 12-game hitting streak from Aug. 31 to Sept. 12.
- Reached 100 RBI with three-run homer off Milwaukee's Chris Bosio on Sept. 30, becoming first Mariner to reach 100 RBI in consecutive seasons.
- Finished third in AL in extra-base hits (70), fourth in slugging percentage (.535), fifth in doubles (39) and multi-hit games (52), sixth in total bases (302) and eighth in batting average (.308) and homers (27).
- Received third straight Gold Glove and finished second among AL outfielders in fielding percentage (.997).

Year	Team	Avg.	G	AB	R	H	2B	3B	HR	RBI	BB	SO	SB
1992	Seattle	.308	142	565	83	174	39	4	27	103	44	67	10

KEN GRIFFEY JR.

1993

- Belted 460-foot homer off Minnesota's Scott Erickson in Kingdome that hit a speaker and caromed into the second deck on May 9.
- Became sixth-youngest player to reach 100 career homers with home run off Kansas City's Billy Brewer on June 15.
- Was AL's top vote-getter for All-Star Game with 2,696,918 votes, second only to the Giants' Barry Bonds.
- Became first player to hit B&O Warehouse at Baltimore's Camden Yards during All-Star home run-hitting contest on July 13.
- Established AL record for outfielders with 542nd consecutive errorless chance in Boston on July 18. Streak ended Aug. 8 at Texas at 573 consecutive errorless chances.
- Began major league record-tying streak of home runs in eight straight games with eighth-inning clout in New York off Paul Gibson on July 20.
- Surpassed Richie Zisk's club record for home runs in consecutive games with his sixth off Cleveland's Jose Mesa on July 25.
- Tied major league record with a home run in eighth straight game off Minnesota's Willie Banks on July 28.
- Broke Gorman Thomas' club record for homers with his 33rd off Kansas City's Tom Gordon on Aug. 10.
- Hit 40th homer off Detroit's Mike Moore on Sept. 1, becoming the first Mariner to surpass the 40-HR mark and the 10th youngest in major league history to reach 40 homers.
- Made first career appearance at first base in Minnesota on Oct. 2.
- Set new club marks in runs (113), total bases (359), homers (45), intentional walks (25) and slugging percentage (.617).
- Led league in total bases (359) and extra-base hits (86), and finished second in homers, intentional walks and slugging percentage.
- Received fourth Gold Glove and second Silver Slugger awards.

Year	Team	Avg.	G	AB	R	H	2B	3B	HR	RBI	BB	SO	SB
1993	Seattle	.309	156	582	113	180	38	3	45	109	96	91	17

1994

- Hit game-winning, 438-foot home run onto Eutaw Street in Baltimore off Brad Pennington, the longest home run ever by a lefthanded hitter at Camden Yards.
- Set club record with 20 RBI in April.
- Hit first home run in Boston on May 3, the last AL city in which he hadn't homered.
- Became third-youngest player to reach 150 homers after connecting off Texas' Roger Pavlik on May 20.
- Took over as franchise leader in career homers, surpassing Alvin Davis, with career blast No. 161 in Texas on June 15.
- Led all major leaguers in All-Star Game balloting with record total of 6,079,688 votes en route to being selected to start in his fifth straight All-Star Game. Finished first half hitting .329 with 33 homers and 69 RBI in 87 games.
- Won All-Star Game home run-hitting contest at Pittsburgh's Three Rivers Stadium with seven dingers.
- Saw streak of 145 consecutive games started broken on July 31 in Chicago.
- Won first AL home run crown with 40 and became 22nd major league player to hit 40 or more homers in consecutive seasons.
- Finished second in AL in total bases (292) and intentional walks (19), and third in runs (94), slugging percentage (.674) and extra-base hits (68).
- Finished third among AL outfielders with 12 assists and received his fifth consecutive Gold Glove Award. Also won his third Silver Slugger Award.
- Finished second to Chicago's Frank Thomas in AL MVP balloting.

Year	Team	Avg.	G	AB	R	H	2B	3B	HR	RBI	BB	SO	SB
1994	Seattle	.323	111	433	94	140	24	4	40	90	56	73	11

1995

- Hit game-winning, three-run homer on Opening Day vs. Detroit.
- Belted a 462-foot homer into the Kingdome's third deck against Detroit's David Wells on April 29.
- Fractured both bones in left wrist making a running catch into the wall in right-center in the Kingdome against Baltimore on May 26. Missed the Mariners' next 73 games.
- Voted as a starter to the All-Star Game for the sixth straight season, trailing only Cal Ripken Jr. in total votes.
- Collected career hit No. 1,000 off Minnesota's Frank Rodriguez on Aug. 16 in his second game back after the injury, becoming the seventh-youngest player in history to reach that mark.
- Delivered his first game-ending hit on Aug. 24 against New York, a two-run homer off John Wetteland.
- Registered his 100th career homer on Sept. 20 off Texas' Bob Tewksbury.
- Took over the lead in all-time Kingdome homers with No. 102 on Sept. 26, passing Alvin Davis.
- Finished the season with a career batting average of .302, second in Mariners history to Edgar Martinez's .312 average.

Year	Team	Avg.	G	AB	R	H	2B	3B	HR	RBI	BB	SO	SB
1995	Seattle	.258	72	260	52	67	7	0	17	42	52	53	4

KEN GRIFFEY JR.

Major League Leaders in the '90s

Average
Tony Gwynn	.341
Frank Thomas	.323
Paul Molitor	.314
Hal Morris	.310
Ken Griffey Jr.	.308

Hits
Kirby Puckett	1061
Tony Gwynn	1047
Rafael Palmeiro	1044
Paul Molitor	1038
Brett Butler	1011
Ken Griffey Jr.	919

Home Runs
Cecil Fielder	219
Barry Bonds	208
Fred McGriff	199
Matt Williams	191
Albert Belle	187
Frank Thomas	182
Ken Griffey Jr.	173

Most Home Runs By All-Star Break

HRs	Player	Club	Year
37	Reggie Jackson	Oakland	1969
34	Frank Howard	Washington	1969
33	Ken Griffey Jr.	Seattle	1994
33	Roger Maris	N.Y. Yankees	1961
33	Mark McGwire	Oakland	1987
33	Matt Williams	San Francisco	1994
32	Frank Thomas	Chicago	1994
31	Willie Mays	N.Y. Giants	1954
31	Kevin Mitchell	San Francisco	1989
31	Mike Schmidt	Philadelphia	1979

STANDING TALL

A.L. Outfielders With At Least Five Consecutive Gold Gloves		
Player	Consecutive Gold Gloves	Total
Al Kaline	7 (1961-1967)	10
Paul Blair	7 (1969-1975)	8
Dwayne Murphy	6 (1980-1985)	6
Dwight Evans	5 (1981-1985)	8
Ken Griffey Jr.	5 (1990-1994)	5

Youngest Players To Reach 150 Career Homers		
Player	Age	Career HR
Mel Ott	23 years, 6 months	511
Eddie Mathews	23 years, 10 months	512
Ken Griffey Jr.	24 years, 5 months	172
Mickey Mantle	24 years, 8 months	536
Jimmie Foxx	24 years, 8 months	534

PHOTOGRAPHY BY TOM DiPACE

A compendium of Junior's achievements and rankings among his peers — both current ones and all-time greats

The Sky's

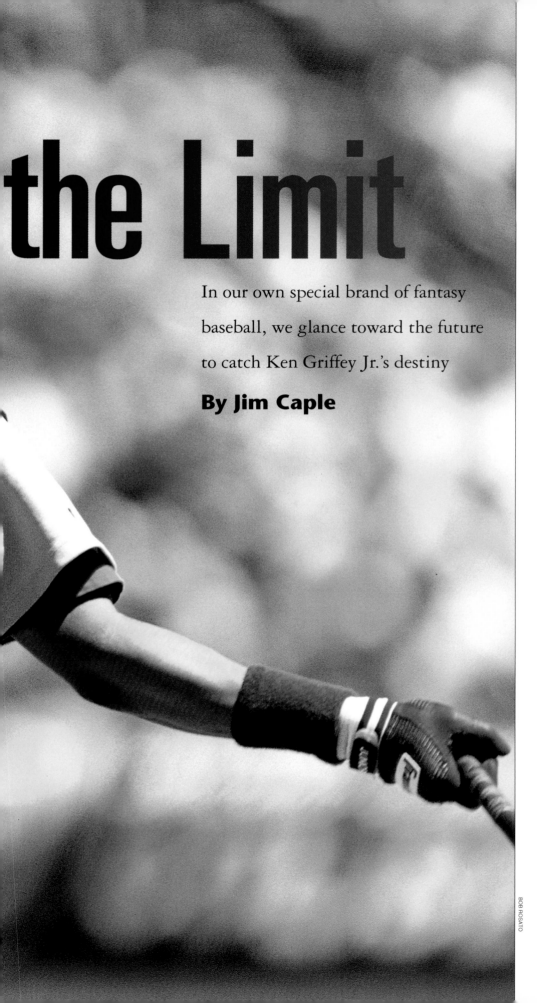

the Limit

In our own special brand of fantasy baseball, we glance toward the future to catch Ken Griffey Jr.'s destiny

By Jim Caple

A t age 26, Ken Griffey Jr. already has had the kind of career most major leaguers envy. With six consecutive All-Star selections and six Gold Gloves to his name, Junior's possibilities are especially mind-boggling. No one can know just how his career will play out through the years, but here's our take on what he will have done by the time he hangs up his Nikes for good.

TOKYO — The circle is complete.

Ken Griffey Jr., who homered in the same game as his father, Ken Sr., more than two decades ago, homered in the same game as his 19-year-old son, rookie Trey Kenneth Griffey, last night during the Nintendo Mariners' 13-10 victory over the Brooklyn Dodgers.

The home runs were the 18th of Trey's young career and the 648th of Ken's.

And as it turned out, the elder Griffey's home run was his last. He announced his retirement immediately after the game in a tearful press conference carried live on ESPN6.

"I've accomplished all I've wanted to do in this game," Griffey said. "I've won the World Series twice, and I've got an Olympic gold medal. I played in All-Star games, set home run records and won MVP awards and a Triple Crown. Now I'm ready to sit back and enjoy my son's career."

Acting commissioner Bud Selig was on hand to congratulate Griffey after the historic game, and he later promised to present a new contract proposal to the players association within a few weeks. Fans watched an interactive highlight video on the TokyoDome's virtual reality board.

"We love Ken Griffey Jr. because he is everything we would like to be," a hologram of Reggie Jackson said in the tribute. "He's young, he's good-looking, he's got the best smile in the world, and he's a heroic athlete. He is a shot in the arm for baseball. He is what this game needs right now. He is creating excitement and making headlines just by his presence."

Jackson originally said those words just before the 1994 strike, better known as the "Short Strike," but his words applied to Griffey at virtually every point of his magnificent 25-season career, during which he transformed from "Junior" into "The Rising Son."

Griffey played in four decades and his career spanned some of baseball's most glorious, volatile and often wrenching times. Thanks to interleague play, he played in all 48 current major league cities and homered in 87 ballparks, from the recently demolished Camden Yards and dingy Old Coors Field to baseball's venerable hallowed grounds, the Metrodome.

In addition to his 648 home runs (fourth all-time), Griffey retires with 3,420 hits (sixth), 2,009 RBI (third), 6,245 total bases (second) and a .322 batting average.

His totals would be higher had his career not been interrupted by three work stoppages. He broke Roger Maris' home run record with 64 in 1998, and probably would have reached 75 had 38 games not been canceled that year by a midseason strike.

But mere statistics alone cannot capture the drama of his career. Griffey not only excelled at baseball, he seemed to personify and carry it as well. Each time a prolonged strike or lockout threatened to kill off base-ball, Griffey helped breathe life back into its lungs, providing some of the sport's most thrilling moments.

"Ever since Junior was a rookie, my line has been, 'And the legend continues,' " former catcher David Valle said during Griffey's eight-game home run streak in 1993 (a streak Griffey surpassed with 10 straight in 2001).

"First at-bat in the majors, double off Dave Stewart. First at-bat in the Kingdome, home run. First pinch-hit, game-winning home run. Then his dad comes along. He singles, Junior singles. Then next week in Anaheim, Dad homers, Junior homers. And now this.

"Man, the legend does continue."

Beginning with his first hit, Griffey provided baseball with many of its most memorable blows:

• His home run off the B&O Warehouse at the 1993 All-Star Game festivities;

• His record-breaking six postseason home runs in 1995;

• His 1997 playoff home run, which was the only ball ever hit out of old Yankee Stadium and the last home run hit in New York City until the Dodgers moved back in 2006 (in 1998, the Yankees moved to New Jersey and the

Junior hit the showers early during the "Short Strike" of 1994, but his charisma and talent helped baseball win back its fans by the turn of the century.

Mets left for Nashville); and

• His 1998 line drive that hit Cal Ripken Jr., putting the shortstop in a weeklong coma and ending his record playing streak four games later.

No stage was big enough for Griffey, not even an international one. Perhaps his most memorable blow was his gold-medal winning home run in the 2000 Olympics. The two-out blast cleared the stadium and struck the Sydney Opera House.

And always, there was that style, that grace.

"Junior always seems to be having more fun than the rest of us," was a frequent comment of Frank Thomas, perhaps the only player who could match Griffey's hitting prowess.

Maybe a little too much fun, at least early in his career. Despite all Griffey's talent, a criticism in his early years was that he did not give 100 percent. Midway through the 1992 season he even announced that running out grounders "was not part of my game."

With maturity, however, that attitude gradually changed until he became one of the most competitive players in the game. He often said the 1995 season

was the turning point.

"Fighting back from that broken wrist was the first real adversity I had to deal with and it made me a hungrier, better player," Griffey said in 2003 after becoming baseball's first $1 billion player — a contract that was considered enormous at the time. "Then getting a taste of the postseason that October taught me how important winning was and left me with only one goal — winning a World Series."

Griffey finally reached that goal in 2001 when the Mariners (then still in Seattle) defeated the Chicago Cubs in seven games. Griffey was named series MVP after hitting .410 with four home runs and eight RBI.

He hit three more home runs in the postseason the next year to become the first player to win the award in consecutive years and earn the nickname that best described his postseason performances: Mr. November.

And now that his career is over, he'll be remembered as something else: The Greatest.

"If I can accomplish half as much as my father," Trey Griffey said in the tearful clubhouse, "I'll be happy." •

Jim Caple covers Major League Baseball for the St. Paul Pioneer Press.

BY THE Numbers

0 hits in 14 career at-bats against Orioles ace Mike Mussina

1 first player selected in the June 1987 free agent draft

2 age of son Trey Kenneth

3 years of football at Moeller High in Cincinnati

4 times on the disabled list in his seven seasons in the major leagues

5 consecutive Gold Glove awards

6 RBI, a career high, June 13,1994, at Texas

7 career grand slams

8 consecutive games in 1993 with a home run

9 runs scored in five-game playoff series vs. New York in 1995

11 straight times reached base safely April 23-27, 1989, setting club record

12 straight games with a hit, the longest hitting streak of his career (achieved four times)

14 two-homer games in career

17 years old when began pro baseball career with Bellingham of the Class A Northwest League in 1987

18 Mariner team records **19** age during his rookie major league season in 1989 **22** home runs through May in 1994, breaking Mickey Mantle's record of 20 in 1956 **26** age of Ken Griffey Jr. **30** number wore in honor of his father on Turn Back the Clock Day in Kansas City on May 21, 1993 **32** stolen bases during 58-game stay at San Bernardino in 1988 **33** home runs at the All-Star break in 1994, the third most in history **73** games missed because of broken wrist in 1995 **102** (not including postseason) career homers in the Kingdome, a stadium record **145** consecutive starts from Aug. 16,1993 through July 31, 1994 **341** home runs by the Griffeys, the fourth-highest father-son total in history behind the Bonds (554), the Bells (407) and the Berras (407) **350** youngsters who attended a Christmas dinner sponsored by Griffey in 1994 **359** total bases in 1993, a club record **462** How many feet his longest career homer traveled, into the third deck of the Kingdome on April 29, 1995, off Detroit's David Wells **1,000,000** number of Ken Griffey Jr. Chocolate Bars sold in his rookie season **16,260,857** total number of votes received in All-Star balloting

Artist Andy Yelenak created this original cover in celebration of *BBCM's* 10th Anniversary (issue #116, November 1994). The commemorative cover features the two players who helped boost the hobby to its present state: Frank Thomas and Griffey Jr.

November 1994
Issue #116

BECKETT
BASEBALL CARD MONTHLY

®U.S. $2.95
Canada $3.95

KEN GRIFFEY JR.

FRANK THOMAS

Hot List Heroes

IC
TH
ANNIVERSARY

Like the hobby he helped revitalize, Ken Griffey Jr.'s baseball career continues skyward. Even before he and his father suited up together with the Mariners, Griffey was smiling on the cover of *Beckett Baseball Card Monthly* (July 1990, issue #64). Nearly seven years later, as Griffey resumes his convincing march toward Cooperstown, *BBCM* looks back at those many wonderful issues that The Kid made so special.

Beckett

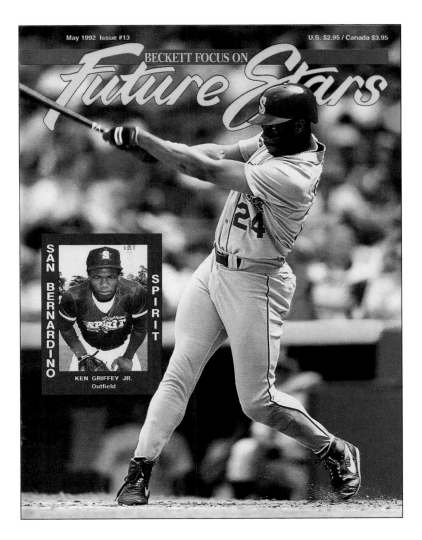

Just three years into his career, the 22-year-old superstar landed a front cover spot on *BFFS* issue #13 (May 1992). His raw talent and potential already had established him as one of the most collected young players in all of sports.

Remembers

Beckett
Baseball Card
Monthly

Issue #64 July 1990 $2.50

Photographer Tom DiPace captured Junior in characteristic form for Ken's first front cover appearance on *Beckett Baseball Card Monthly* midway through his sophomore season (issue #64, July 1990).

Imagine not being able to go out to the mall, video store or dinner without being hounded by a group of well-intentioned folks who want you to sign 'just one more' autograph. No dinner goes uninterrupted, and everything you do or say is analyzed. That's the easy part. For Ken Griffey, the real work is

the Job
of being

Junior

by Bob Finnigan

July 1995 BECKETT BASEBALL 7

Griffey's latest appearance under the *BBCM* masthead (issue #124, July 1995) not only features him on the covers and inside with a detailed feature, but it also contains a story on Junior's high-profile sports card history and an eight-page comic in which he combats an evil video-game demon.

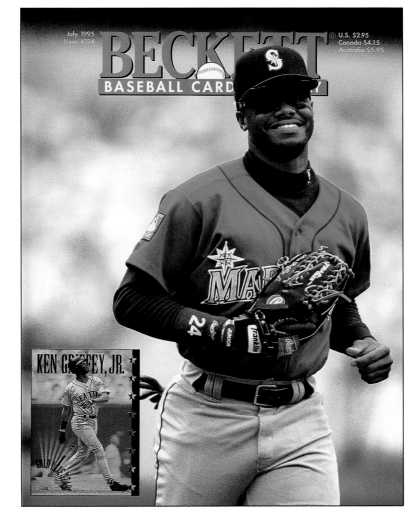

Already a regular to *BBCM* readers, Griffey graced the inside back cover of *Beckett Focus on Future Stars* issue #4 (August 1991).

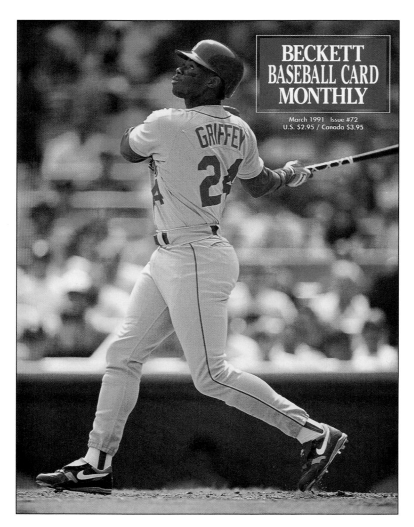

*B*BCM issue #72 (March 1991) kicked off the 1991 baseball season with Seattle's All-Star center fielder on its front cover.

Four years into his career, Junior's popularity continued to rise. His front cover appearance on *BBCM* issue #95 (February 1993) caught him on the heels of his third consecutive 20-home run season.

As a No. 1 draft pick, Ken Griffey Jr. lived up to his lofty expectations. Other No. 1 draft picks throughout the years however, weren't quite so lucky. This *BBCM* feature examined the impact other top draft choices have made in the majors (*BBCM* issue #111, June 1994).

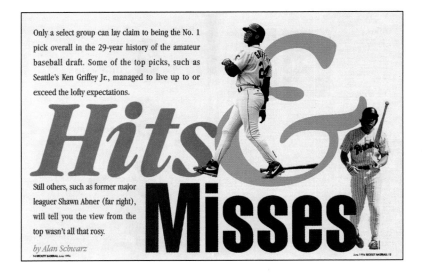

Only a select group can lay claim to being the No. 1 pick overall in the 29-year history of the amateur baseball draft. Some of the top picks, such as Seattle's Ken Griffey Jr., managed to live up to or exceed the lofty expectations.

Hits &

Still others, such as former major leaguer Shawn Abner (far right), will tell you the view from the top wasn't all that rosy.

Misses

by Alan Schwarz

Leading the pack for 1989 Rookie of the Year honors at the time, Griffey Jr. appeared on his first *Beckett* cover sans his trademark smile (*BBCM* issue #53, August 1989). He also reported in as No. 1 Hot in that issue's "Weather Report."

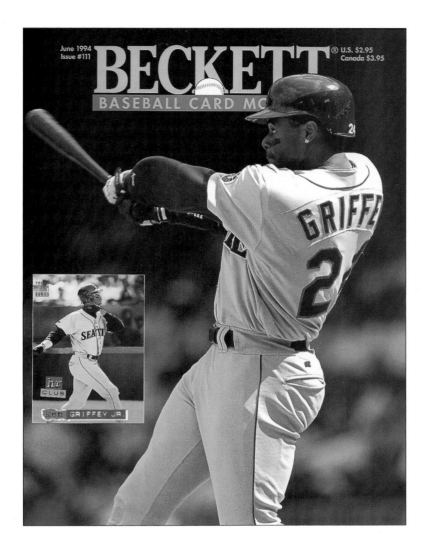

BBCM issue #111 (June 1994) presents Junior's trademark swing on Cover 1 for his third *Beckett* front-cover appearance.

Equally productive with a Sharpie in hand, Griffey satisfies dozens of autograph hounds as pictured in *BBCM* issue #97 (April 1993).

BECKETT GREAT SPORTS HEROES

DON'T MISS THE WHOLE NEW LINEUP!

They are household names, and their performance on the court or field has made them legends. Just a mention of these extraordinary athletes brings to mind the epitome of grace under pressure, courage, persistence, and the highest levels of sportsmanship.

Beckett Publications and House of Collectibles are proud to celebrate the top sports heroes of yesterday, today, and tomorrow with the continuing series of Beckett Great Sports Heroes.

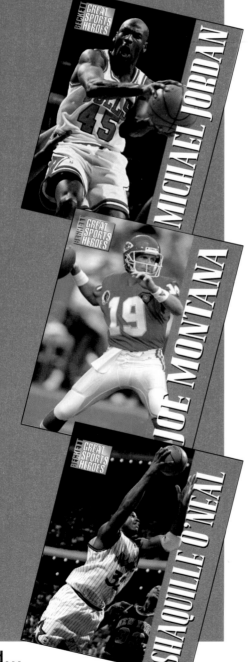

Look for these exciting titles wherever books are sold…